Wild Thing

Escapades of a Bunbury Boy

Rob Britza

A catalogue record for this book is available from the National Library of Australia

Copyright © 2021 Rob Britza
All rights reserved.
ISBN-13: 978-1-922343-70-3

Linellen Press
265 Boomerang Road
Oldbury, Western Australia
www.linellenpress.com.au

Dedication

For my children: Tim, Cath and Jamie
my stepchildren Kieran and Selena
and all my wonderful grandchildren

Contents

Dedication iii

Contents v

Introduction 1

Part One 3

Memories of my Father 3

    Hubert Edward Britza 4
    War Service 7
    War Service Medals 9
    Carpenter 10
    Smoker 10
    Bicycle Racer 11
    Fisher 13
    Shooter 16
    Mechanic 20
    Handyman 24
    Garage and Workshop 30
    Dad's Last Years 32

Part Two 35

    Mum 38
    Our house 45
    Rear Block 46

Household Services *49*

Barry *52*

Warren *58*

Dixie *61*

Donna *63*

Nana & Grandad Britza *65*

Grandad Forster *69*

Nana and Pop Howson *71*

Part Three **74**

Primary School *74*

High School *78*

Part Four **81**

Entertainment around Bunbury *81*

Around the Houses Road Racing *97*

Bunbury Shops *98*

Daredevil *100*

Aunties and Uncles **104**

The Forsters (Mum's Grandmother and Uncles) *104*

Uncle Pat and Aunty Judy Forster *109*

Uncle George and Aunty Betty *111*

Aunty Lorna (Mum's sister) and Uncle George *112*

Aunty Hazel (Mum's sister) and Uncle Ted *113*

Uncle Bill and Aunty May (no relation) *114*

Aunty May (Mum's Aunty) and Uncle Bill *114*

Uncle Jack and Aunty Vi (Mum's first cousin Vi) *115*

Uncle Don and Auntie Dot (no relation) 115

Uncle George and Auntie Norrie (no relation) 117

Mr and Mrs Staley (no relation) 119

Cousins 119

Graeme Kenny 120

Brian Kenny 121

Janice Nash 122

Johnny Hay 124

Pat O'Brien 125

Glen Britza 126

My Cotton Cobra 138

Working for a living in my teens 141

Mothers Day 1964 145

Rehabilitation 148

Part Five 156

Bunbury Characters 156

Arthur Dunn 156

Jim Moon 157

Judy Moon 158

"Halfpenny Harry" 159

Learning to Drive 160

My first cars 161

Acknowledgements 165

About the Author 167

Introduction

I decided some time ago to write 'memories of my father' because my eldest son Tim had asked me about my Dad; what he was like, what he worked at, what hobbies he had, and the like. This took me by surprise as I assumed my kids would have no interest in my past or that of my family.

As I was thirteen years old when Dad died, I thought I would have few memories of him, but to my amazement, as I jotted notes down, more memories popped into my head. As I wrote these memories down, I remembered I had some photos of Dad, both recent (just before he died in 1960) and older photos showing him at work, with his cars, siblings, and with Mum when they were courting. Some of those photos I have included in this book.

Along with my memories of Dad and the family came many memories of my childhood and teen years growing up in South Bunbury.

The idea came to me that as our lives and activities in the fifties and sixties differed so vastly from our kids growing up in the 70s, 80s, and now our grandchildren, I should add memories of my childhood to the story. And, of course, I have many photos of us growing up and using some of the toys and other interesting and dangerous things we played with.

I hope my kids, grandkids, extended family, and friends will enjoy reading about my upbringing and the adventures of my teen years, which were at times funny, informative, sad, and most of all, interesting.

Part One

Memories of my Father

Dad holding me

Hubert Edward Britza

Born in Bunbury, Western Australia
To parents:
George Frederich and Elsie Nellie Britza (nee Ytting)
On the 24th of May 1919
Died on the 4th of May 1960 from Nephritis
Buried in the Bunbury Cemetery
in grave number 40, Methodist section

Me at Dad's grave

Mum & Dad's wedding

Dad married Joan Agnes Forster on 17th of August 1942

Dad at 23 months old (1921)

Aunty Dora, Dad, Uncle George in 1919

War Service

Dad enlisted in the RAAF (Service No 45247) in 1941 when he was twenty-two years old and was discharged in 1945.

On the 14th of August 1942, while living in Como with her Mum and sisters, Nin and Hazel, Mum received a telegram from Dad saying he was coming home so they could get married while he was on embarkation leave. He was about to sail to England, and would later return to Australia on an aircraft carrier.

They went to Bunbury, received a special licence, and were married. After a ten-day honeymoon touring around the South West of Western Australia, they returned to Como. Dad then returned to Adelaide.

When he arrived there, he found out the trip to England had been cancelled, and in 1944 he was posted to Darwin. Two weeks before Barry was born, Dad was posted to Adelaide, so he didn't see Barry until he was seven months old.

Mum said that, while Dad was in Adelaide, he told her he was going to a four-year-old's birthday party, so she asked him what age the kid's older sister was. Mum said he sent her photos of his girlfriends over there, so she decided what was good for him was good for her, and started going out with other blokes over here.

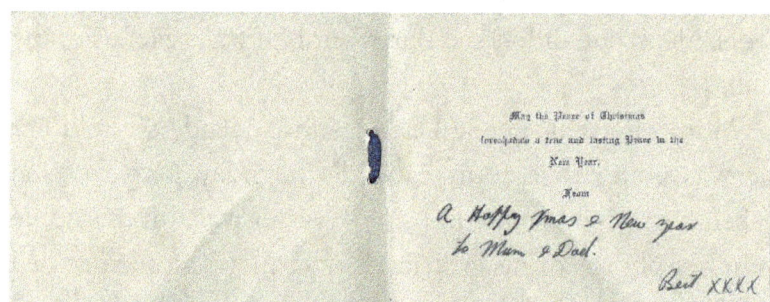

Dad sent the Christmas card above to his parents sometime during the Second World War.

War Service Medals

Dad was awarded two service medals, which I have in my possession. I have worn them to ANZAC parades, including in Rockingham, Darwin, and at the end of our driveway in 2020 during the Coronavirus pandemic.

The first time I marched on ANZAC Day with Dad's medals pinned on my chest was in 2013 at Rockingham. I've had the medals for many years and had them re-ribboned and mounted on a bar so I could wear them.

As I approached the 'form-up' point, I felt apprehensive, but at the same time, for the first time in my life, I felt Dad was with me. It was an odd feeling, yet despite this, I felt out of place among all the other people wearing their medals or the medals of their forebears.

I had previously arranged to meet a mate there who marches every year so I had somebody to talk to and feel comfortable with amongst all these heroic survivors of so many military conflicts.

During the march, both sides of the roads were packed four to five deep with thousands of people applauding and photographing the marchers, including me.

I felt out of place and a big fraud for being there among these others but, while approaching the assembly area for the service and laying of wreaths, I, with Dad's help, realised it was right to be there. I realised the applause wasn't for me – it was for the medals on my chest and the memories of what my father and the others went through in their conflicts.

Carpenter

Dad was a carpenter, a trade he learned on the job – without an apprenticeship – with Ausden & Prosser, Millers and house builders in Bunbury. He resumed employment with Ausden & Prosser after the war, as a carpenter and foreman until he resigned due to sickness in 1957.

He often came home for lunch and, being young, I was in awe of him sipping his tea from his saucer. I guess he did that to cool it down enough to drink it in time to get back to work.

I was always amazed at his skill and speed when sharpening his pencils. He used a pocketknife for normal pencils and a sharp chisel for his flat-shaped carpenter pencils.

Every December, Ausden & Prosser would hold a 'Carpenters Picnic' on the Busselton foreshore, which was a real treat in those days. There were all sorts of games and sports played, including one where contestants had to lean down and put their head on their hand on top of a small pole, then turn in three circles. When the circles were completed, the contestants had to run to the next pole. Much to Mum's amusement, Dad got dizzy and spun off into the ocean.

Smoker

Dad smoked 'roll-your-owns' using *Champion Ready Rubbed* tobacco. Before a car trip, he would roll several smokes and have them up on the internal sun visor so he could grab one and light it as he drove. He gave me one to try when I was about six years old while we waited for the chip heater to heat the water to run a bath. I nearly choked and didn't try again until I was about eleven years old.

That time I was with a mate, Tony Edwards, and he got me to try a fag behind the Forest Theatre in South Bunbury. The same horrible result, so that was the end of that potential bad habit.

Dad was a real 'Ocker', as were most men in those days, and used the words 'cobber' and 'bonser' all the time.

Bicycle Racer

Dad raced bicycles and competed at various venues, including Busselton, riding to many of these venues as practice and exercise. I can remember one trophy he won, which is now in my brother Warren's care. There used to be a velodrome of sorts in Bunbury around the oval near the beach on the town's northern end. He took me there to watch some bike racing, but I don't remember seeing him race there. Maybe by then, he had finished competing.

He rode a pushbike to work and most other places around Bunbury. It was a fixed wheel bike – that is, the rear sprocket didn't ratchet so kept going around. They were a mongrel thing to ride because as you leaned into a corner, you had to stand the bike up a bit every time the inside pedal approached the road. I assume that is how they raced bikes in those days. Gears on bikes must have been invented many years later.

He used to dink me around on his bike, and he taught me to ride my first bike, which I received on my fifth birthday. It had stand-up cow horn handlebars and back pedal brakes. I wanted to drop the handlebars like all the racing bikes around town, but Dad wouldn't let me. This was probably for safety reasons so I wouldn't race around head down, arse up, not watching where I was going, and run into something. He told me about a bloke who was killed on his racing bike because he wasn't watching where he was going and ran into the back of a tractor parked on the side of the road.

So my bike wouldn't get stolen while I was at school, Dad arranged with somebody living on a corner near the school, for me to open their side gate and park my bike in their backyard for the day. I never once saw anybody at that house, so who lived there is anybody's guess. I often wonder if those people even knew about me or wondered who the hell was hiding a bike in their backyard.

Me with my first bike at five years old

Me wearing one of Mum's hats

Fisher

Dad enjoyed a bit of fishing, and I remember well the first time he took me fishing. He bought Barry and me our own lines, made of green twine, and took us fishing on and under the Bunbury Jetty. I was incredibly young and doubt if I could even swim at the time, and here I was with Barry and Dad climbing down vertical ladders to the beautiful and deep green sea. Even now, I can remember the colour – it was awesome. The rail-less beams we walked on under the jetty would only have been about 250 mm wide and were slippery because water often washed over them. There we fished with the sea surging and lapping the beams we were on. Was he trying to get rid of me at that early stage in my life?

Mum did a lot of fishing, from the top of the jetty, as we kids often did too. One day I was only catching Trumpetfish and grew annoyed with it, so the next one I caught I threw away as hard as I could. Silly me. I threw it back tail-first, and the spines on its back stood up, pierced and broke off in my index finger and the edge of my palm. When I got home, I tried to push the spines back out with a sewing needle poked through the skin at the other end of the spine. Good idea and a bit painful, but it didn't work. I put up with them for a year but finally got fed up when I couldn't catch a cricket ball or do a lot of other things with that hand without a lot of pain. I rode my pushbike to the hospital and had the spines removed under a local anaesthetic and rode home again. The scars are still visible sixty-odd years later.

We also went fishing at a spot on the Collie River called *The Bend* at Australind. Mum also went with us, probably because it was safer than under the jetty. As young kids, we soon grew bored and just ran and played along the river bank, including climbing in and out of boats people had tied up on the bank.

As we grew older, we would ride our pushbikes to the jetty to go fishing. When we reached our teens and could ride further, we also rode with all our fishing gear, out to *The Bend* to catch bream, a distance of about twelve kilometres each way.

We did a lot of crabbing using scoop nets at various spots along the Leschenault Estuary at Australind. One day we had Aunty Hazel (Mum's sister) and her family with us when Aunty Hazel was bitten on the toe by a crab. She jumped backward and landed on the edge of the galvanised iron bath she was using to tow around behind her to put the catch in. Because we had caught heaps of crabs and the bath was half full, angry crabs were going all directions with Aunty Hazel screaming her head off. Oddly enough, nobody ran to help her – we were all cracking up too much.

At one spot at Australind, there was a lot of, what we call, 'sergeant ants'. These ants were about 25 millimetres long with red and black segmented bodies and big fangs which stung like buggery. You can imagine the pain as, besides not having shoes, we didn't wear undies either.

Speaking of undies, it's a good thing I didn't wear any as a real young kid as one day walking down to Nana Britza's place, I had an accident and had some objects falling out of my pants. I just kept going and watched the dogs following me eat up the lumps – bloody dogs will eat anything. I had a similar incident many years later as an early teenager while at the motocross track watching all the action. I had an urge to rush to the bush and do some business there but wasn't quick enough. Knowing that undies cost a fair bit, and not wanting to get into trouble for losing them, I cleaned them up as best as possible with leaves and then rolled them up and shoved them down my shirt until I got home. I tended to keep my distance from other people in case they got a whiff of something, but nobody looked at me sideways, and I couldn't smell anything myself.

There were a few pieces of clothing I hated as a kid, but

don't know why – I just did. The first was braces on my shorts, and I've never worn them since, not even in fancy dress. The second was singlets, and everybody wore singlets in those days. Then there were sandals: what a dumb piece of footwear they were and still are as far as I'm concerned. I think they're called sandals because when you get within five kilometres of the sand, the 'sand all' gets in your shoes.

When I first went to school, Mum would comb my hair with the part in the middle. Holy mackerel, did I hate that? As soon as I was out of sight, I'd mess it all up.

Shooter

Boom! Boom! The shotgun blasts echoed around the Ferguson Valley, making the nearby leaves shake and all the animals and birds hurtle for cover. Except for one. Out of the sky tumbled the most graceful of Australian birds – a magnificent 2.5-metre wing-spanned Wedge-tailed Eagle. Dad and Uncle Ted gleefully ensured the 'nemesis of lamb farmers' was dead, and proudly dumped it in the back of Dad's ute. The intrepid hunters then brought their prize kill home to South Bunbury and showed off their prowess as hunters and champions by ridding the skies of the most hated scourge of the South West.

Unfortunately in those days, kids were told they had to be 'seen but not heard', so there was no point showing my feelings about the bird, and I would've just been laughed at and told to 'get over it'. Many years later, I reminded Uncle Ted about this episode. He was not pleased with himself any longer, but remorseful about it.

Dad owned several firearms, including a shotgun used

when spotlighting – or 'spotting' – for roos. Somebody would drive the ute while he stood in the back, and somebody else in the passenger seat held a 'spotty' aimed into the bush. I also keenly took my turn at this job. The roo's eyes would reflect red and the spotter would yell "Stop!" and Dad would then shoot the roo. If the roo didn't die first up and we could find it, it was finished off and then gutted. The smell of hot roo guts is something I will never forget, and I was intrigued by a part of the gut that looked to me like a pumpkin.

At home, the roo was hung up to bleed out and then cut up into steaks etc. Roo tails were used by some people to cook 'Roo-tail Braun', which I never tried because I thought it looked disgusting.

One night we got a big buck, and when we reached home, it was gutted and chopped up. Uncle George (Dad's older brother) kindly presented me with the roo's scrotum and testicles, which I carried in my pocket for days. I thought they would be a good luck charm, despite not bringing the roo much luck. Well, I *was* only about eight years old!

Dad and Uncle Ted were very close-knit brothers-in-law, both particularly good shots and proud of their rifles of which they had several each. Dad, being a carpenter, made gun cases for their favourite rifles. Both he and Uncle Ted cleaned and polished their rifles religiously after each outing.

Another 22-rifle Dad owned had a telescopic sight. He also kept that in a wooden case he made especially for the purpose. This rifle was used for competition shooting in the Bunbury Small Bore Rifle Club where the shooters would lie on the floor, and a bipod was used to steady the end of the barrel to shoot at targets. The competition was held in the Bunbury Rowing Club on Sunday nights and I remember Dad won lots of trophies, usually spoons.

Dad (right) with his brother George return from hunting

Dad also had a .22 rifle for hunting rabbits, which we did at dusk. When we saw a rabbit while driving along a road, we'd stop, and Dad would shoot it. If the rabbit was moving before Dad shot, he would give a short sharp whistle and the rabbit would stop for an inquisitive look and a bullet.

I remember one hunting trip when the whole family went on a picnic in our Prefect ute, with Uncle George and his family in their car. We were in the hills in the Ferguson Valley when suddenly Dad and Uncle George came running into the clearing yelling at us to get in the cars because a mob of wild pigs was coming our way. Seconds later, a mob of ugly boars and sows ran through our picnic area while we kids watched from the back of the ute.

Another hunting excursion was to shoot foxes who were

– and still are – vermin. In those days there was a bounty to be had from the Agricultural Department for their demise. Hunters would shoot the foxes, cut off their ears, and present them to the Department for the bounty. Also, foxes tails were often used as decoration on car aerials for all to see and admire.

Foxtail on car

The shooting wasn't the only method of bringing food to the table. Dad also had a lot of rabbit traps which he would set in rabbit burrow entry holes during the late afternoon. Early the next morning, we would go back and pick up the rabbits from the traps. The rabbits would still be alive, and he would hit them over the back of the head to kill them, and then gut them on the spot and skin them at home.

He made a small steel hoe slightly wider than the trap to dig out the dirt to bury the trap under a couple of millimetres of dirt. He did this after laying a piece of newspaper on the tripping plate to stop dirt from interfering with the mechanism. After laying the trap, Dad would hang a piece of newspaper or toilet paper in a bush near the burrow.

"Why are you hanging that paper there?" I asked, thinking that other people would see it and know there was a trap there and pinch it.

"So we can find all the traps tomorrow," he replied.

I was happy with that logic as it made sense to me – I don't think I would've found them again without the paper.

The rabbit traps were spring-loaded devices with teeth that grabbed the rabbit by the leg and held it until the hunter returned the next day. To ensure the rabbit didn't dive back into its hole and take the trap with it, a spike about 300mm long was attached to the trap with a chain and driven into the ground. Those traps are now banned because they are very cruel to the rabbits.

Mechanic

Dad was a bit of a mechanic and worked on his cars a lot, as you needed to in those days. He built a large set of wooden ramps in the back block that he drove the car onto so he could walk around under the car to service it. The ramps' uprights were big logs, the ramps themselves must have been about 300 x 150 mm in section, with two side by side for each side of the car and 4 metres long.

The motors of at least two old utes in the yard that he got from somewhere were used for his circular saw. These utes were an A-model Ford and a T-model Ford that didn't have starter motors like today's cars, so they had to be cranked to start – a laborious job. After fitting the engine to a metal stand he'd made, he fitted a pulley about 200mm wide to the motor's crankshaft. This drove a long flat belt about 3 metres to another pulley on the spindle of the saw bench. Sometimes the pulley would slip inside the belt, so he would spoon some golden syrup (looked and tasted like honey) on the inside of the belt to make it grip.

There were several of these circular saws around South Bunbury and on Sundays (men worked six days a week then) you could hear these saws 'singing' as men sawed up wood. This was a distinctive sound which everybody recognised. Above the saw and motor, he built a large roof which must have been 10 metres by 10 metres and was enclosed on two sides. This shed also doubled as a woodshed where he stacked tonnes of firewood as he chopped it up.

There were also some old car radiators in the yard, which as a young kid I wrecked with a hammer because I liked the way the water dribbled out of the holes I made.

These old cars were great to play in and pretend to drive. They had wooden spoked wheels and the throttle and choke levers on the steering column. It's a shame I didn't get photos of those vehicles and his ramp.

The next image is Dad in his beloved *Tin Lizzie* with somebody I don't recognise.

Judging from the number painted on the door, the crash

hats they are wearing, and what looks like a reporter with a microphone, I'd say they were competing in some sort of race, or other, motoring competition.

Dad in car with racing number on side

Dad had a few other cars, including his Ford Prefect ute which he built a canvas-covered canopy on the back of, in which we kids used to travel. He fitted a 12v light in the canopy so we could see what we were doing during night travels. This we loved as we would've been bored without a light. According to Mum, Dad had a mania for cars and owned fifteen in his and Mum's eighteen years of marriage.

A kid I don't recognise, Barry, me, Warren, with a Vauxhall and the Prefect with canopy on the rear

Barry with me in a pram

Mum, Barry and me with the Prefect sedan

Handyman

Dad was always making things, including a large icebox. When we were kids, the family didn't have a fridge – most people didn't – so Dad built a big, wooden icebox that stood on the back verandah. He drilled a hole in the bottom of the icebox; drilled a corresponding one in the floor, through which the melted ice would run out into the sand under the house. The 'Iceman' would come around once a week and deliver big blocks of ice for the iceboxes. He would carry the ice inside using a large ice tong and separate the blocks with an ice pick.

Dad made wooden louvres for toilet windows and sold them to who I don't know, but at a guess, it may have been to builders.

He also built a wooden trailer that he used to cart firewood and anything else he needed to move around. In those days, trailers weren't required to have lights, so he didn't fit any as he (hopefully) only used it in daylight. Later, one of my mates, Donny Collins, borrowed the trailer to cart his motocross bikes to a race in Perth, and he fitted lights to the trailer.

I was in a play at school playing a woodcutter or something, and I needed an axe. Dad made me one of the double-edged types out of wood with sharp edges. The teachers were impressed, I'm sure, with me waving this thing around on a stage full of kids. But hey, those days safety was never thought about.

Another thing he made was a washing trolley for Mum to wheel the washing out to the clothesline. It had a round steel tubular frame and handle with the wheels and the body all made from wood.

He sharpened all his tools by hand, including his handsaws and circular saws. He had a commercially available 'saw set' which he used to set the correct angle on the teeth of his handsaws, but he made up a circular wooden jig to hold the circular saws. He would hammer the saw's teeth down to the correct angle and then sharpen them with a file.

Dad also assisted Uncle George (his brother) to build his new house in Forrest Avene in Bunbury. Another house he assisted with was Aunty Hazel and Uncle Ted's place in Carlisle which was a direct copy of the layout of our house.

Dad with Barry and me in a wheelbarrow Dad may have made

Dad built me the flashest hill trolley in town (shown with Donna).

My hill trolley had a steering wheel, wooden wheels, and a foot brake which operated on the rear wheels. I used to race the trolley on hills in a new subdivision south of our house. The land had been owned by an old bloke named Vickery who used to harass us to try and get us off *his* land. One day we must have annoyed him too much and he called the traffic cops (run by the Bunbury Town Council).

One of the cops, Jim Moon, turned up on his motorbike, and kids scattered everywhere. I wasn't going anywhere and leaving my prized hill trolley behind, so I just got a stern talking to. The parents of the other kids got a letter from the Council, but not my mother. Jim used to go to school with Mum, and I think he was still scared of her.

Another part of our backyard was fenced off for a vegie patch. To make his fertiliser, Dad put chook manure in a 200-litre drum and kept the drum topped up with water. He would use a bucket to take the enriched water out of the drum and pour it around the vegies which grew vigorously.

About a year before Dad died, Don Wendt bought him an electric bench saw to use as a hobby and to make things to hopefully sell and make a few bob. One day while he was using it, Warren walked in and inadvertently distracted Dad for a second. In that second, Dad cut one of his thumbs straight down the middle to the first knuckle. His thumb looked like a ging prong and eventually healed, but always looked ugly after that.

He died within several months of that, and unfortunately, Warren being only eight years old when Dad died, for some time blamed himself for Dad's death.

From left; Brian Kenny, Warren, Barry at rear and me with my "Bodgie" outfit and pushed back hairstyle on the seesaw Dad made for us

Alongside the rear of the house, Dad built 'the bike shed', which was about 6x3 metres and where we housed our pushbikes. It also had other stuff built into it including three large boxes where we stored our daily firewood supplies of differing sizes. My job was to keep the boxes filled, which I did by using a kiddie trolley with four wheels to bring the firewood from the woodshed.

I used to climb to the top of the bike shed and jump from it to the roof of the house, a gap of about a metre, but when I wanted to get down again, I just jumped off the house roof onto the ground. The house and shed roofs were both made of asbestos which was strong and not likely to be broken by my weight. I could climb over the roofs if I kept a safe distance from the power cables going to the shed and coming in from the power pole out the front.

Under the house was an adventure as well, and being a small kid, I could get to any part of the house between the stumps. One day I found a dead snake under there with holes in it – it must have been bitten by our cat. Dad reminded me that our cat had been extremely sick for a few days but recovered, and he suspected that the snake had bitten it during a fight.

Dad with his kids before he got sick.
Barry, Warren, me, Dixie in front C1953

Garage and Workshop

Dad built a shed in the backyard with power and lighting, which was radical for those days. The shed was separated into two sections by a wall across it with a doorway in the wall. On one side of the wall was the garage to house the car, and the other side was his woodworking workshop where he made things using his woodworking tools and machinery. The wall on the workshop side was his shadow board where his tools hung.

Along one side of the garage side was a workbench for when he was working on the car and the other side was all shelving for parts, tools, and oils etc. On one end of the workbench was a foot-operated grinder, which you pedalled like buggery to keep the wheel going while you ground away at whatever you were sharpening.

Under the workbench were all sorts of mystical things including an old steel trunk that held what, I don't have a clue. There were hundreds of strange things in the shed, but as a kid, I didn't know or care what they were.

As was the norm in those days, the house and the shed were built on stumps, and to get the car into the garage, it had to be driven up a ramp. When I imported my motocross bike from England at sixteen years old, I used to ride it up the ramp into the garage. The first time I rode it up the ramp I gave it too much throttle and flew off the top of the ramp into the shed. As I was going through the air, I had both wheels locked up with the brakes, but when I landed, I skidded straight through the wall showering tools from the other side of the wall all over the place. Mum got a bit upset for some reason and threatened that when I got a house and a shed, she was going to ride a motorbike through the end of my shed. I laughed at the mental picture of that, but she didn't need to, because my first son Tim did it for her.

Tim on his 50cc Honda embedded in my shed wall

When Tim was about six years old, I bought him a 50 cc Honda motocross bike; he had a track around the backyard and behind my sheds. One day I was inside the house and Tim was tearing around his track when I heard a loud crash and a wail. Tim had got out of control and put his front wheel through the side of one of the sheds. I raced outside and could see he wasn't hurt, so told him to stay exactly where he was while I got the camera to take a photo to send to Mum in Bunbury. She was suitably impressed.

Dad's Last Years

Dad had been suffering from Nephritis for about three years and was unable to work, but Mum never told us kids that he was likely to die – she may have told Barry because he was the oldest, I don't know. She had only told us that Dad was very sick and that he would be in and out of hospitals, but not one word about him one day not coming out of the hospital alive.

When Dad died, Mum immediately started calling Barry 'the man of the house now'. This annoyed and frustrated me because Barry was less than two years older than me; he was a bully to me and nowhere approaching being a man, in my opinion.

As far as I'm aware, Dad first got sick when I was ten years old. As the sickness and infirmity worsened, we kids just carried on like nothing was happening, as we were not told otherwise.

Dad wrote a few letters to us while he was in the hospital, and he once sent three stamps to us so we could write back to him with our news. Being unaware of the imminent dire position Dad was in, and receiving no encouragement from Mum to write back, we just ignored it. I remember thinking at the time that I should write back, but I didn't, which now when I think about it makes me sad. We may have thought at the time: "Why bother? He'll be home soon."

During the last months of his life, Dad was bedridden, so Mum bought him a small bell to ring when he needed anything. I remember her exasperation at times when he rang the bell, which upset me and made me sad as he couldn't help being sick and needing help. Hence, at the time I thought she was being selfish. In her defence, I realise now, she was bringing up five kids and running the house as well as taking in ironing, she would have been run off her feet.

Dad by now was constantly itchy all over and, according to Mum, it was because "his kidneys were not working properly and his 'wee' was coming out through the pores in his skin." I don't know if that was a fact, or if she was just making it up, so we kids had an answer. Of course, as a thirteen-year-old, I naively believed everything my mother told me regardless.

As the end drew near for Dad, family and friends would drop in to ask Mum "how are things going?", which made her break down and cry. By now, I had worked out for myself that Dad must be close to dying, despite still not being told by any of the adults around us. We were of the generation that was told many times; "kids should be seen and not heard" and "go outside and play".

I must have annoyed Dad too much one day not long before he died, and he told me to "get lost" so I jumped on my deadly-treadly and took off to get lost. For me, that was an impossible task as I knew Bunbury like the back of my hand, and even if I'd ridden off into the bush, I would've found my way back home anyway. So, I just slunk home and kept out of trouble for a while.

One day I asked Dad what made the thunder, and his reply was "it's the clouds running into one another", which I believed of course. I guess my parents were not as learned as we were to become, or maybe the schools they went to were second-rate if indeed they even attended school enough?

I was home on the day Dad died. Mum and Aunty Dora

(Dad's sister) returned from the hospital after watching him die. The postman had just been, and I rushed over to Mum and Aunty Dora with a letter, saying "There's a letter here for Dad."

Aunty Dora took the letter from me and said: "I'll take that." There were tears behind her sunglasses and I knew then that my Dad had died.

Aunty Hazel came down from Perth to help Mum with stuff, and she is the only person I remember trying to console me. I can still remember sitting on the front steps of our house when she, unfortunately, made the mistake of offering consolation in the form of "God only takes the best." This made me feel angry, hurt, and disappointed. *How could God take good people and leave bad people behind?*

I didn't say anything, just kept the thoughts to myself, as we were taught to do.

For several months I quietly cried myself to sleep, as I had nobody to console me or talk to about how I felt. I had to cry quietly as Barry and I shared a bedroom, and I knew if he heard me, he'd tease me. I have no idea how my siblings felt and coped, as nobody in our family spoke about or were encouraged to talk about their feelings. There was never any compassion or empathy in our family for anybody.

The thing that burned me up terribly, and I can now see this affected my relationship with Mum, is she wouldn't let me go to Dad's funeral. I was thirteen years old for God's sake! I was going to ride my pushbike to the cemetery, but I was so scared of Mum I didn't. I have lived to regret not doing that. Decades later, after harbouring my feelings, it occurred to me this made me feel bad toward Mum.

Part Two

Three months before Dad died, Mum gave birth to a girl. I found out many years later that this created a furore among Dad's family.

Aunty Dora asked Mum, "How could this happen?" meaning that, as Dad was so sick, the child could not possibly be his.

I was there at the time and clearly remember Mum's sarcastic retort: "The same way it usually happens!"

There was no love lost between Mum and Aunty Dora, which I was unaware of until decades later.

After waiting years for Mum to do it and not getting it done, Aunty Dora had a headstone placed on Dad's grave. Mum was angry monumentally about that and had the cemetery people remove it and had another one made. Unfortunately, the new one had a mistake on it, and it's never been corrected. It showed too little time between Darrel's and Warren's birth dates on the headstone, so Darrel had been born the year before that which is shown on the headstone.

I visited Aunty Lorna (Mum's youngest sister) and spoke at length about all this. She told me she and all the family and friends knew all along that the baby wasn't my Dad's as he 'couldn't get it up'. Aunty Lorna's daughter Georgina was with us during this discussion. She told me that she and all the other cousins knew about it too as they grew old enough to be told and understand.

Something Aunty Lorna told me about Mum made me laugh, knowing my opinion was the same as hers. She said that Mum was a 'street angel' but a 'home devil' as she always put on a sweet front for outsiders but was a demon with close family. Mum also had a 'posh' voice she'd put on if she thought she was talking to somebody she thought was higher class than her, which amused me no end.

She, unfortunately, had what I term 'inverse snobbery' when she'd say of somebody else, "She thinks she's better than us." This baffled me because I couldn't see what she was talking about and didn't think it was correct.

Just before the baby was born, my parents were undecided on what to call it. We spent a lot of time on a farm near Collie owned by 'Uncle' Don Wendt. Don had been helping our family out a lot, including buying Dad a saw bench so he could use it to build toys and other items as a hobby while he was sick. Aunty Lorna told me during our conversation that Don had been helping with money and in 'other ways'.

During a trip to Don's farm one weekend when I was twelve years old, we were discussing the naming dilemma, so I suggested: "As Uncle Don helps us out so much, if it's a girl, why not call it Donna after him?" Dad knew the baby wasn't his and was probably aware that it was Don's baby, but despite this, when the girl was born, she was duly called Donna. Dad took Donna in as his own and proudly showed her off to all his friends and families. This would have taken a lot of guts and understanding that most men wouldn't have or be able to find.

Aunty Lorna told me that Dad told Mum his name could be on Donna's birth certificate, providing she promised never to tell anybody the truth. Decades later, Mum couldn't admit the truth to anybody, despite most people knowing or suspecting the truth.

Dad with his "daughter" Donna

Donna tells me that long before her Dad Don died, they had discussed her parentage and she was okay with that, but not with Mum's attitude and insistence that my Dad was Donna's Dad. When Don died, he stated in his will that "to my daughter Donna, I leave the house in Capel."

And so it was, that after Donna's Dad had died and because of his will, Mum then told Donna that Don was indeed her father.

What sort of mother, thinking that her daughter knew no better, would tell her daughter that her real father had just died? Imagine how Donna would've felt if she hadn't known the truth – it's mind-boggling. Despite knowing the truth before Don died, Donna still, to this day, understandably can't forgive Mum this deceit.

After Don died, my brother Barry and I decided to organise a Forster family reunion from Mum's Dad, Percy's descendants down. I bought a family tree software package to build and print the tree for showing at the reunion and made two versions. The first with my Dad as Donna's Dad and the second with the true parentage shown and asked Mum to choose which version to display. Even then, some years after Don had died, she chose to show the world the lie.

Mum

Mum never mentioned Dad to me until forty years after he died. I was driving her somewhere at the time and had upset her by driving the car way I did. She broke down crying, and said: "I wish your father hadn't died."

I was so gobsmacked by the revelation that she spoke of

his death and that he may have mattered to her, that I was utterly speechless and couldn't respond. I just drove her home sedately and nothing was ever said about it again.

Had she been a more honest and upfront person, I might have been able to talk to her about Dad and my feelings, but it would've been a waste of time trying. She wouldn't have understood my feelings, she'd have lied, and certainly would show no compassion or empathy.

It still hurts that she never spoke of Dad to us kids, it's as if he never existed. Even when I started writing memories of Dad for my kids, she wouldn't give me any ideas to write about.

After Dad died, Mum had to learn to drive the car, so she got Uncle Clarrie McManus to teach her; she duly got her licence and was mobile again. I went to town with her driving the car one day, and we parked outside the Prince of Wales Hotel in Stephen Street. As she parked, she hit one of the verandah posts holding up the cantilevered roof, busting the left headlight.

This amused me greatly, but I made damn sure Mum didn't see me smiling or I would've been in big trouble; yet again!

Mum's Metters No 2 stove was alight all day during the winter and most days during the summer. During the winter, we'd stand in front of it to keep warm and, as kids, we'd all sit around it at night with Mum while she knitted and sung to us. To light it, we used kindling and cut up squares of rag which were soaked in diesel in an open twenty-litre drum at the other end of the toilet. Firestarters were invented decades later. We were brought up to call kindling "mornings wood", I suppose because that's when the fire was always lit for the day. Mum cooked some memorable meals in the old Metters, including roast lamb, beef, chicken, duck, pigeon, kangaroo, and rabbit. They were all cooked in dripping and accompanied by a delicious gravy made with the meat fat, dripping and a bit of Gravox chucked in.

Mum in her kitchen

Some other food we ate in those days included camp pie (aka tinned dog), sausages with mashed potato, polony with butter spread on it, and potato pie. Mum also cooked a fantastic rice pudding for dessert, which we had lashings of fresh cream on.

On occasion when Mum returned from shopping, she'd have some lollies or chocolates which she'd count out to share with us. One for Barry, one for Robert, one for Warren, and one for Mum until the supply ran out. What a treat! It didn't happen often, but when it did, we all lapped it up.

Before Dad made a hot water system by fitting a hot water pipe into the stove, we heated water in a 20-litre copper urn on one end of the stovetop. The urn had a tap on it, and we used the hot water for washing up etc.

Dad fitted a coil of copper pipe to the stove which went to a longer pipe and up into a storage tank on top of the roof. The storage tank was mounted above the kitchen, near the window, and had a 'shepherds crook' overflow pipe fitted to it. When the tank boiled over, the water would shoot out of the crook, hit the roof and bounce passed the kitchen window which confused all our visitors on bright sunny days because they thought it was raining.

My poor mind is still etched with the picture of Mum while we were catching shrimp to use as fish bait. We used to visit a billabong on or near the property belonging to the Johnston family who had a dairy and supplied milk around town. We had small scoop nets made with mosquito netting around a hoop on a wooden handle to catch the shrimp. Mum would roll her dress up and tuck it into her big baggy undies she called *Bombay Bloomers* with the crotch hanging down between her legs!

I got a lot of hidings when I was a kid and as far as I can remember they were only handed out by Mum. She used a lump of wood on me one day, and other days I copped a belt or rope. This was just part of life and I made the right 'noises' to end the punishment and went on my merry way.

I realise now I was constantly trying to win approval from Mum. I used to collect stamps and one day walking to Nana and Grandad's place I saw a pile of letters in somebody's letterbox which I was tempted to pinch for the stamps. When I got home, I told Mum how I'd been tempted but resisted and she immediately gave me a stern lecture about pinching mail. I thought I should have been praised for doing the right thing, so after that, I didn't tell her much about what I was doing. I would've only been about seven years old at the time.

Another day Mum and I were doing something on the kitchen floor, me with no pants on, and I did something athletic and asked her if she could do it. Her response was "Don't be dirty." I was about five years old and didn't know what she was talking about, and to this day I still can't figure out what she may have thought I was doing or what I did wrong.

We read a lot of comics in those days and they always had ads in them flogging stamps etc from around the world. The Phantom comics advertised Phantom rings with the skull and red jewel eyes. I too was a big Phantom fan so had to have one of those and sent away for one. It was a prized possession, so when not wearing it, I kept it wrapped up in cotton wool inside a matchbox for safekeeping. Unfortunately, being very light and not rattling when anybody picked it up, it disappeared never to be seen again. It probably got burnt in the kitchen stove or was thrown out. I was devastated. I whinged to Mum who told me "You shouldn't have put it in a matchbox, you silly boy," and that was the end of it. No compassion in our house!

Many years later, when Mum had emphysema and was attached to an oxygen bottle, I was standing at the stove, which was cold at the time. I quietly farted, then turned around and pretended to sniff the firebox and said, "Bloody hell, Mum, there's a dead rat or something in there. She came over, took a big sniff, and said, "You dirty bastard." Great! Got her again, with everybody having a good laugh.

While she was attached to the gas bottle, I would sometimes stand on the hose where she couldn't see me. She didn't wake up to me as she didn't notice the lack of air being blown in her face, but Dixie abused me. More amusement for all who watched it happen.

Racism was bred into us back then. If Mum ever saw us put coins in our mouths, she'd berate us with "Don't put that in your mouth – a nigger might have had it in his mouth."

All Aborigines were niggers to a lot of people in those days. If Mum had known one of my best mates at school was a half-caste, she would've had a fit, I'm sure. I also didn't tell Mum that I'd been into that mate's house and met his Aboriginal mother.

She had some funny ideas; like during a thunderstorm I'd look out the window at the lightning which I loved doing, and she'd say "don't look at the lightning through the glass, it'll make you go blind."

When any of us got a bad sunburn or a burn from something else, she'd put butter on it to make it better, which of course is heavily frowned on today.

Mum also made a poultice using (I think) soap and sugar, which she bandaged on to us to draw out pus caused by boils, splinters, or whatever.

Mum hated school as a kid and didn't have much time for it, telling me often how she'd wagged school. Despite gaining scholarships for me in high school, she didn't do anything to make it easy for me to study. I had to use the kitchen table with all the other kids going silly around me, so little wonder I started to lag behind my classmates when I used to keep up with the best. I initially enjoyed the homework we were given and would get stuck into it as best I could under the circumstances.

Unfortunately, I had a bit of a problem with algebra so one of my cousins, Jill Hay, would come and give me some tutoring. That didn't last long for some reason, maybe she gave up on me or maybe the noise and mayhem got to her.

Eventually, the lack of study and encouragement suited me, as once I was hooked on motorbikes, all I wanted to do was leave school, get a job, and buy a bike, which I did.

Mum was a really bad loser with a quick temper, which came out when she was playing draughts with Don. As he was about to finish her last men off, she would grab the game board and throw it at Don yelling "You long-nosed bastard." This sort of behaviour and worse should have devastated us kids, but we were used to it, and it was like water off a duck's back to us. Nobody else outside our close family ever saw this behaviour as Mum had split personality disorder down pat, and all our cousins thought she was the best Aunty in the world.

Recently I was watching my son-in-law with his son, aged ten, curled up with each other on the lounge, and it suddenly dawned on me that never had my parents cuddled me or told me they loved me, which made me feel sad watching how it should have been. Being 'seen and not heard' was a way of life, but now I can see how it affected me in so many negative ways.

Our house

Dad built our house on the corner of Minninup Road and Halsey Street in South Bunbury in 1951. The brick veneer house had an asbestos roof, which was replaced by a corrugated iron roof in the 90s. Two steel poles holding up the porch roof at the front were unpainted and rusty, as you can see, until the 90s when Don had them painted.

Our house at 51 Minninup Road, South Bunbury.

Above the left window of the house is something that looks like a TV antenna but is a metal fitting that carried the power wires in from the street.

In the right window, you can see a little white square with a red dot in the middle; it was put in the window on a specified day of the week if you wanted dry-cleaning done. *Fowler's Dry Cleaning* would pick up the clothes, dry-clean them and return them on the same day the next week.

To the right of the house was the shed. The chimneys above the shed are on the roof of the house behind. Our house and shed were demolished and replaced with three small units in 2013, after Mum died.

I was utterly besotted by motocross, and the Bunbury Motorcycle Club and did my best to help with promoting the club and its events. I made up a sign using a sheet of black painted ply with white lettering to hang on the front fence when there was going to be a motorbike scramble on. I got some carbon paper from a sidecar mate who ran *Rumbles Pharmacy Supplies* and wrote out advertising brochures for the events and placed them under car windscreen wipers in car parks.

Our toilet walls were asbestos sheeting and were painted with whitewash – this was a powder that came in cardboard boxes and was mixed with water to make paint. Being a grub, when I was small and my finger went through the toilet paper, I'd wipe any poo off my finger onto the wall. These marks were on the wall for years and eventually were painted over. Amazingly, nobody ever asked what the marks were or how they got there.

Rear Block

We kept chooks and Muscovy ducks to eat and for their eggs, which we would collect every day. Dad built two chook yards to house the chooks, and each chook yard had a three-sided shed for them to shelter in with laying boxes and roosts to sleep on. We used to feed the poultry each day with bran and pollard mixed with kitchen scraps. The chooks would eat anything and loved crab scraps. They used to break up the crab shells and eat them as well, so we probably had the healthiest and hardest eggshells in town. To keep the chooks from flying away, we would trim the ends off the feathers of one wing.

The ducks, however, being too heavy to fly, used to range free around the back yards which meant their eggs were sometimes hard to find. When Barry and I found what we somehow knew were rotten eggs, we would climb up the peppermint tree out the back and pelt the stinking eggs at kids riding passed on their bikes. What bloody ferals we were. Imagine what would happen these days; we'd be in court, and our parents would be sued for damage to clothes and the mental anguish their kids were put through.

Our gings looked like this one but we cut up car tubes and tied that rubber to the prong with string

Once when I was the only one home, I decided to have a bit of fun scaring the ducks. When they walked passed in a procession, I shot a few rocks near them with my ging, but they didn't seem at all fazed. My next shot hit one on the head and knocked it out. Holy mackerel, thinking that I'd killed the duck, I thought I'd be dead when Mum got home. To my relief and amazement, after about five minutes, it stood up, shook its head, and staggered off to make a full recovery.

The rear block had tonnes of timber stacked in it, no doubt pilfered from building sites Dad worked on. Barry and I used to build cubbies out of this timber, old corrugated iron sheets and anything else we could lay our hands on. We built free-standing cubbies – including one with a square hole as a window – underground cubbies, and treehouse cubbies with the timber.

Some of the timber was secondhand and had nails sticking out of it. This was nasty because as we ran around on top of the timber with no shoes on, we'd often have a rusty nail stab us through a foot. Thank God for tetanus shots.

We were adept at making things as kids, including fishing sinkers. We collected old bits of lead from somewhere, melted them over a small fire in the back yard, and poured the molten lead into holes we'd drilled into bits of wood. They were successful and were appreciated by Dad when he went fishing.

We had a pet rabbit for a while and when it died, Barry made a small wooden coffin for it and buried it in the back yard with much aplomb; he even built a cross to mark the spot he buried it. Every week he'd dig it up again to see how much it'd decomposed until it was just a skeleton, and then he was happy and left it alone.

We built canoes using old sheets of corrugated iron which we held together at the ends by bending the ends over and sealing them with tar and then took them to creeks and lakes to paddle around. Being secondhand sheets, they had holes in which we also patched with tar.

Household Services

The postman delivered the mail on a pushbike and when he left mail in our letterbox, he would blow a whistle, so we knew we had mail.

Other services and deliveries available in those days included having our milk delivered daily by Johnston's Dairy. The 'Milko' would carry his churn of milk in and fill up our saucepans at the front door , and as he left, top-up his churn from our front tap.

The milk was very rich and, as it sat in the fridge during the day, the cream would rise to the top of the saucepan and we would scoop it off. My favourite treat was to cut a thick slice of bread, spread lots of jam on it, and soak the whole lot with fresh cream, I can still visualise and taste it today.

The tastiest bread ever was delivered as pure as you like, with no preservatives and other rubbish like today's bread. It was delivered by a bloke on a cart, pulled by a horse that didn't stop. The horse would just keep plodding along while the baker ran from one side of the road to the other, stopping at the cart to pick up the loaves as he went.

We had a metal box with breathing holes in it for the

baker to place the bread in. The bread was still warm when delivered and I can still remember its smell now. Of course, the bread was in loaf form only; you had to cut it yourself. Everybody had breadboards and bread knives in their kitchens for this purpose. Now and again we'd run alongside the baker's cart yelling out for a free bun, and amazingly he would sometimes throw some to us.

To make things easier for the housewives of the day as most didn't drive or have a car, an open-sided truck came around once a week, the driver selling fruit and vegies. He weighed the produce on a set of scales hanging from the roof of the truck. The customers would walk around the truck picking out the fruit and vegies they wanted, which was then weighed, paid for, and of course, taken away in brown paper bags or boxes.

Underwood's Grocery Shop in Bunbury had a service that was second to none. Mr Underwood came around on a Tuesday and took the housewives' orders and delivered the groceries the next day. They sold all sorts of things besides groceries, including some hardware. Mr Underwood had a son, Eddie, who eventually took over the order/delivery role. He was a genuinely nice bloke who would sometimes join us for a cup of tea. When he visited Nana Britza, he used to wind her seven-day clock for her because she couldn't reach it where it was above the stove. I guess that was only after Grandad died, as he would have wound the clock himself, being taller than Nana.

One service we didn't have in the house at Minninup Road, but Nana and Grandad had, was a removal service, not a delivery. Once a week, the dunny man would come and remove the dunny pan (or shit can) from the 'thunderbox' through a little door at the back of the outhouse. He would replace it with a clean, empty one that had a wooden seat box above it for a toilet, hence the name 'thunderbox'.

Most houses had a dunny lane behind the back fence so the truck could get as close to the dunnies as possible, but for some reason, Nana and Grandad's block didn't have a dunny lane. The 'shit can' was a drum with a capacity of forty-five kilograms when full. The Sanitary Engineer, or Dunny Man, would carry the drum of sewage on his shoulder to the truck.

The Dunny Man

Barry

When I was four years old and Barry was six, we were collecting cigarette butts to get the tobacco out to make cigarettes for ourselves. We chopped them up with a rusty old tomahawk and, as one butt rolled off the chopping block, I pushed it back just as Barry brought the tomahawk down. There's not much to a four-year-old finger so there it was, hanging by a small piece of skin. He was a good shot as there were no bones damaged as the tomahawk went cleanly through the knuckle.

According to Mum, we had previously been playing a pirate game and I had a sock and hook on my right hand, which is why I used my left hand to move the butt. Little wonder I never smoked.

Barry took off to our grandparents' place to hide, and Mum yelled out for Dad while she held herself up by leaning her eight-month pregnant body on the clothesline. Now knowing Barry and his sadistic tendencies growing up, I wouldn't be at all surprised if he chopped my finger off deliberately.

Being a weekend, we couldn't find a doctor to stitch me up, and we ended up at the Bunbury District Hospital in Parkfield Street which was demolished decades ago. When I asked them what they did with the remains of my finger, I was told they fed it to the hospital cat!

Uncle George Britza's first comment was: "You'll have to use another finger to pick your nose now," which amused me greatly, and I haven't looked back since in the nose-picking game.

We used the same chopping block to chop off the chooks' heads when Mum needed a chook to cook. Barry and I would chop off their heads and pluck them, then Mum would gut them and cook them. To catch the chooks, we used a crabbing scoop net and, after catching them, would reach under the net to grab their legs to carry them with.

Several years later, Barry put a pick through the back of one of my hands while we were digging a hole. He was swinging the pick while I leaned my hand on top of the shovel handle, and when he swung the pick over his shoulder, it hit the top of my hand. It was an accident that time, but I bled a lot just the same, and I had a scar that lasted years.

When I started school, I terrorised the girls by pointing my stumpy finger at them and making them scream and run away. I also had a trick to make people nearly faint. I cut a hole in the bottom of the inside of a matchbox, lined it with cotton wool, and poked my right index finger through to rest on the cotton wool. With mercurochrome on that finger and also my stump, I'd open the matchbox up and show my seemingly severed finger in the box and my stump on the other hand.

Barry was very much a bully and didn't mind who he bossed around. One day, I came into the lounge room with my cousin Glen to play some of Glen's records on the gramophone. The records were of the sounds of bikes racing around the Isle of Man, with a commentary on who the riders and bikes were. It lasted about five minutes then Barry ordered us out saying: "If I wanted to listen to shit like that, I'd go down to the swamp and listen to the frogs."

Barry and his mate one day found a litter of newborn kittens and decided to have a game of cricket with them.

They took it in turns to bowl a kitten to the other, who would hit the kitten for a six with the cricket bat. They also had a plastic bag with something in it another day, that they wouldn't show me. I hate to think what it may have been if it was too nasty to show me.

He made a small guillotine one day so that when he shot a silvereye out of a fig or mulberry tree and it didn't die, he could lie it in the guillotine and while humming a death tune, drop the blade and cut the bird's head off. Very entertaining but macabre.

Our chooks and ducks bred well, but unfortunately, one clutch of chickens was being killed off by a feral cat. Barry decided we should do something about it, so one night when Mum wasn't home, he found a dead duckling and placed it in the unused chook pen with four rabbit traps set just under the dirt and surrounding the duckling. That night from inside the house, we heard a cat screaming, so jumped up and ran down the backyard to where Barry had hidden a couple of long pieces of wood, and we beat the cat to death.

Barry loved being cruel to animals, and one day as I came up the back ramp into the verandah, he yelled out: "Hold the door open." I didn't know what he was up to, so did as I was told and next thing, with one kick, he had booted our cat from the kitchen, across the back verandah, and out through the back door.

While the house was being built, we had an outback dunny which, when the house was finished, was used to store the bags of bran and pollard that we fed the chooks with. There was also a wooden tea chest there that we mixed the bran and pollard in, and the mixing stick leaned in the chest. We discovered that while the door was closed, mice would get into the chest and as the door opened, they escaped up the stick and jumped off onto the ground and away. Barry's next sport was for one of us to open the door quickly and the other beat the mice to death with a length of timber as they tried to escape.

I remember getting my revenge back on Barry only twice: once when he had me down sitting on me and trying to tickle me to death, and I head-butted him and made his nose bleed; the other time was at Aunty Lorna and Uncle George's place in Cannington where he was chasing me around and bashing me. I was hiding from him and, as he peeked around a corner of their house looking for me, I picked up half a house brick and timed it perfectly. I threw the brick when I thought he'd poke his head around again and bang, got the mongrel fair in the forehead. He left me alone for the rest of that day.

Barry had an Italian girlfriend name Carmel for a while until one day while he and Carmel were talking outside her house, Carmel's father came out to warn Barry. He scared Barry with: "You stay away from my daughter, or I shoot you, Italiano no fucka da English."

Never one to take risks, Barry kept well away from Carmel, and according to Mum, Carmel's father had already been in trouble for stabbing another bloke at the Picton Pub.

I nearly wet myself laughing one day when Mum and I, for some reason, drove to where Barry's girlfriend Carmel worked to talk to her. A bloke came out to see what we were after and Mum said, "I'm looking for Carmel Dunn." Carmel Dunn was the best-known prostitute in Bunbury at the time, and Mum's gaffe broke me up.

Turkey Point was a favourite destination for Barry. It had a tennis court, and tearooms, which were a popular tourist destination from the early 1900s to the 1950s. Many people spent summer days there. A ferry – the *Valdemar* – ferried two loads of passengers a day there during the holiday season. I never did go on it because, by the time I was old enough to go, the service had stopped. Turkey Point is the south side of the 'cut', and all the buildings and tennis courts disappeared many years ago. You can now drive through the area without knowing there had been an oasis of holiday fun there.

Barry was a member of the Bunbury Youth Club for a while and had a ball playing up with some of the girls in the club. The youth club had a bonfire night in November, and he enjoyed telling me about the stupid things they did; throwing crackers and aiming skyrockets at each other.

The CMF (Citizens Military Force) attracted him for some time as he enjoyed going away for weekend bivouacs, wearing a uniform, and firing an Enfield 303 rifle which he could keep at home. They met one night a week where they undertook training and marching.

Unusual for Barry, instead of bullying me, he saved me from drowning twice. The first time was in a deep hole in an empty block alongside the drain that ran out to the sea. I fell or stepped in and Barry dragged me out. The second time, we were swimming at the Baths. The deep end of the jetty had a couple of platforms, and the shallow end one platform. These two areas were about ten metres apart. As a superhero, but not able to swim at that stage, I thought I could dive in from the deep end, hold my breath and kick my way underwater to the shallow platform. Wrong again! I came up halfway and started to flounder, so Barry saved me again – my big brother coming to the fore again when needed!

Most years a circus came to town and we managed to see it a couple of times when we had the entry fee. At one performance as the elephants came into the big top, a dog frightened an elephant and it panicked and took off. Unfortunately, it hit and knocked down one of the big posts holding the tent up, which dropped toward the crowd opposite us. People started running for the exit. We saw it all happen, which was exciting for me, but poor Barry jumped up to run and shit himself, so we walked home with his shorts full of his mess.

He took me out for my first attempt at catching prawns using a dragnet one night. As we were walking along the Estuary, I felt something slide passed my leg and into the net. Next thing, the end of the net was jumping up and down out of the water. I nearly panicked and wanted to hit the shore saying: "Shit, there's a crocodile in the net."

It was just an enormous cobbler that swam into the net and was eaten by the family later that week.

Barry bought a lawnmower after he'd been working for some time, and I used it to cut other people's lawns, towing it to the people's houses behind my pushbike. He never asked for any payment for using it, and I never even gave it a thought either. I used his lawnmower to cut our lawn as well, pretending it was a motorbike racing into corners, revving it up and down as I went.

Barry (right) and me   *Barry and Donna*

Warren

For some time, when I arrived home from school, Warren would be outside the gate waiting for me, and one day I decided to scare him by riding at him, but braking just before I hit him. Unfortunately, I mistimed it and ran into him. He never waited outside for me again, which made me feel sad and guilty about being a dill.

He was known to fall asleep anywhere, and one night Aunty Hazel came out into the kitchen to get us to go have a look at him in the bath. There he was lying face down with his head on the sloping end of the bath, sound asleep with his mouth just above the water.

Years later when he was about fifteen years old, we were

at a party in the kitchen of a house we were visiting when a drunk Warren leaning up against the side of the fireplace, fell asleep standing up. What a legend!

In my 'Bodgie' fad and, seeing what the bodgies in England were getting up to, I decided to make a chain out of short lengths of rusty wire twisted together, and whipped Warren around the legs with it. He screamed with pain and had some minor bleeding from some scratches, but we cleaned it up before Mum came home and I didn't get into trouble for that effort. Barry's sadistic ways were now rubbing off on me.

Mum took Warren down the jetty one day to do some fishing, but he got ahead of her and disappeared into a shed on the jetty. He came running out immediately, followed by a big Negro. Warren told her the bloke called him into the dark shed, and when he got in there, the bloke grabbed Warren's hand and put it on the bloke's penis. Mum took off after the bloke screaming at him: "You black bastard!" She was ignored, of course, and the bloke kept walking up the jetty to his ship.

Warren is five years younger than me and into motorbikes too, although he never raced them in motocross. He competed in enduros and, while living in Northam, started up the *Avon Trailbike Club* which ran enduros in the bush near towns around Northam. He left Northam for Yanchep, where he and I often rode together in the bush around the national park and sometimes through the national park. Together, we marked out a successful enduro for the club just north of Yanchep, beginning at a picnic area called *Jarrah's End*, where the jarrah forest ended its northerly run.

Warren, Dixie and me with the pedal car

There were lots of roos and emus in this area and we loved to chase them until they veered off the track into the bush. Emus were the worst to chase because their large feet kicked up lots of dirt, so it was lucky we wore goggles to protect our eyes.

One day we came across a patch of something growing with a rabbit-proof fence around it; probably marijuana, so we got out of there quickly.

Warren had a strange mate when at Primary school -

when he visited, he didn't knock on the back door like most normal people; this kid would sit on his pushbike out in the backyard and bark like a dog. Warren would bark back at him, mount his bike, and away they went on their bikes to whatever adventure they had on that day.

We all know what a great fisherman Warren is today, but when he was a kid it was a different story. He used to ride his pushbike to go fishing on the jetty with his mate, Terry Lockwood, who lived next door. Terry always came home with a big bag of good fish, but Warren could only manage a few, most of them blowies.

Dixie

Warren, Dixie, and Donna on one of the hill trolleys we made

Dixie joined us boys one day at our dirt track (which would now be called a BMX track). I, unfortunately, came to regret inviting her along. One part of the track had a gully in it where we'd ride down one side on a slope and up the other side on another shorter slope. Alongside the slopes were vertical drops of about 1.5 metres and, as we approached, I was about to overtake Dixie on her right, when she heard me coming up behind her and moved over to the right to give me room to pass on her left. If she'd stayed on course, I would've passed her as we went down the slope, but now I had nowhere to go except over the edge. I escaped with no injuries or damage to my bike but gave her a verbal lesson on what to do when somebody is approaching from behind.

She had to give Mum a lesson in modern language one day when arriving home from high school. She and a friend were walking home from high school via a path between houses when a bloke stepped out to give them an eyeful. When she arrived home, Dixie said to Mum: "We saw a wanker today."

"What's a wanker?" Mum said, so Dixie had to explain to Mum what the bloke was doing.

Some people chew their fingernails, but Dixie went one better than that and chewed her toenails. She denied this of course, so one night I sneaked up on her armed with my camera and got some proof of her disgusting habit. I passed this photo onto her daughter and grandies, who were suitably impressed with their gross Mum and Nana.

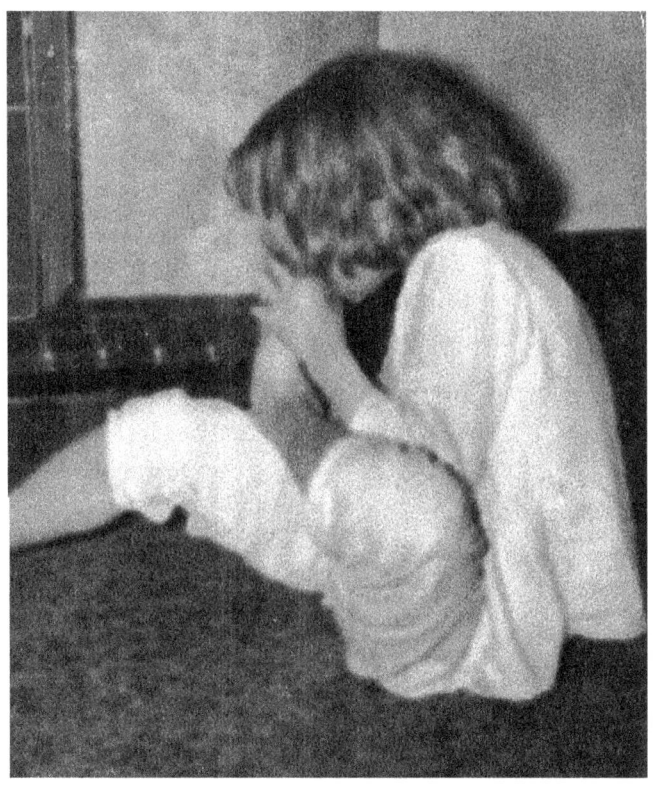

Dixie chewing her toenails while watching TV

Donna

I had a special affinity with Donna as my baby sister, and played with her at every opportunity, taking lots of photos of her with my Brownie Box Camera. As she grew big enough to hang on, probably around two years old, I proudly dinked her on my pushbike all over Bunbury, visiting friends and relatives.

We sometimes had a bath together, which meant a lot of splashing and making a mess of the bathroom, but we had a lot of fun and enjoyed ourselves.

After my motocross accident, while wrestling with

Donna on the lounge before I had my badly dislocated shoulder reconstructed, my shoulder would dislocate if I lifted my arm above elbow height. There was no pain involved; I just shrugged my shoulder up while jerking my elbow toward my ribs and the shoulder would re-locate. Donna was none the wiser and we just carried on roughhousing each other.

She was devastated when I had to go to Perth to live during rehab and only coming home on the odd weekend, and of course, I missed her too. But we had a lot of fun together when I was home.

Donna and me

Warren, Dixie, Donna on the wooden rocking horse built by Dad

Nana & Grandad Britza

Nana and Grandad lived in Latrielle Road, South Bunbury, just a few hundred metres from us, and, as a kid, I spent countless nights with them sleeping overnight. There were no radios or TV in the house, so we all used to chat and read. I read their bible most nights, and for my eleventh birthday, they gave me my very own bible, which I still have. I went to Sunday School for a while and took my bible, but that went by the way as there were more interesting things to do on a Sunday morning.

On hot nights we'd sit out on their front veranda to keep cool and had our feet and lower legs in cloth sugar bags to ward off the mosquitoes.

Nana and Grandad's house in Latreille Rd, Bunbury 2015

Because the dunny was so far down the backyard, I had a china potty under the bed to wee in during the night. Before I got the potty when I went outside for a wee, my imagination ran away with me and I thought a crocodile would get me, so I'd just wee on the grass near the back door. Another crocodile in Bunbury?

Nana and Grandad's outback dunny, still in use in 2015, but now with a flushing toilet

They also had a spare block at the rear of their property, and it also had stacks of timber in it which I suspect was also pilfered by Dad. Living in the stacks of timber was a feral cat and her kittens, which I befriended. When they trusted me to play with them, I stole one of the kittens to take home as a pet. I made a house out of bits of timber from our rear block so the kitten would feel at home, and eventually it became tame and a good pet.

Grandad used to shave using a cut-throat razor, and I remember the sharpening strops hanging up behind their bathroom door. It was intriguing as a small kid watching him strop his blade and use it with shaving cream spread over his face.

The only car of Grandad's I can remember was an Austin A40. It had leather seats that gave off a great odour I can still remember. One of Grandad's sheds had a pit in it for driving the car over so he could get under it to service it. The driveway from the road to the shed was a two-wheel rutted path through the buffalo grass, and believe it or not, it was still the same when I visited in July 2015.

Grandad had about four sheds, including one that was open on one side and had firewood and other stuff stored in it. Out the front of that shed was his 'sawhorse', a timber device used to hold the wood while it was being sawn. He sawed it with a long two-handled crosscut saw that I sometimes 'helped' him with while cutting up logs for firewood. Years later, I made my own sawhorse the same as his, but of course, I used a chainsaw to cut up my logs.

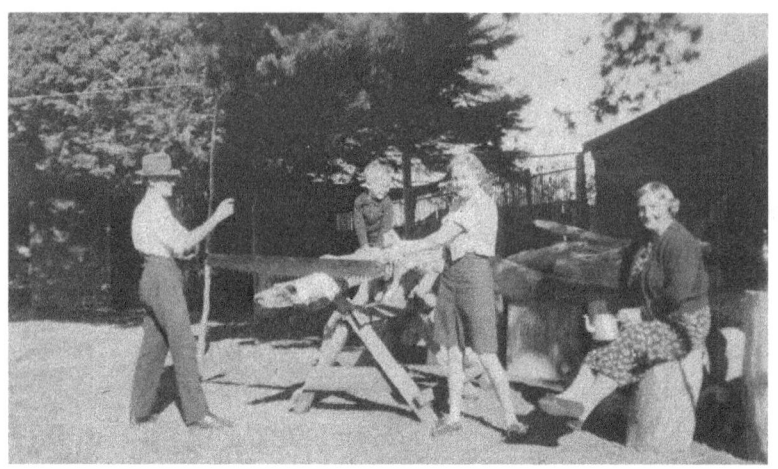

Grandad Britza on the left, Aunty Betty on the other end of the saw, Nana Britza on right

Grandad always moaned about having to pay water rates despite not being connected to the mains, which ran past the front of their house. They had a windmill and tank on a high tank stand in the backyard for groundwater, and four or five other tanks down the side of the house for rainwater, so they were self-sufficient.

Their house had lots of old, framed photos hanging on the walls, but they wouldn't tell me who all the people in the photos were. I guess it may have been because the war had not been over for long and they didn't want to talk about our German family connection. Who knows?

All the tanks, and the windmill, are now gone, but amazingly, the current owner – who bought the property when Nana died – kept in place the windmill pipe coming out of the ground, to a metre high. He coincidentally was the ice delivery man who delivered our ice and who I mentioned earlier.

Some of Grandad's sheds are still in existence, so is his

greenhouse where he grew his herbs and other small plants. The original bath is now being used as a garden bed, and the original outback dunny is still in use, albeit with a modern cistern and bowl.

Nana and Grandad with their Austin A40 and our dog Jip

Nana's kitchen was often a remarkably busy place as her daughters (Aunty Dora and Aunty Betty), with their kids, visiting often. Usually, they were all talking at the same time. Nana sometimes had fruit cake on hand, and I used to get stuck into that. It's still my favourite cake. She also made awesome scones which I scoffed with lashings of jam and cream – another of my favourite meals to this day.

Grandad Forster

Grandad Forster, aka Old Percy – Mum's dad – was a mean old bastard who disliked kids and was disliked by all us kids. He was never employed a day after the Second World War, but was on a Totally and Permanently Invalid pension (TPI pension) despite having nothing apparently wrong with him. He didn't have a house of his own so lived with us or Uncle Pat Forster and Aunty Nin Kenny at different times. All the kids in those families disliked Percy as much as we did, and Graeme Kenny, like me, used to give Percy a hard time as well.

Percy was a cook in the Army during the war and was posted to Palestine for some time. While there he had one of their paper money notes printed with his and his kids' photos on it. That note is now in Donna's care.

Before the war, he worked for some time on the railway line to Mornington Mill which the timber trains used to haul the cut timber to Bunbury for loading on to ships, but I don't know what his job was.

On pension week, he would go to Perth on the train leaving early morning and returning in the evening on the return train, both called *The Shopper*, because it took people to Perth daily for their shopping. Mum reckoned he had a girlfriend in Perth, but who knows? He probably frequented brothels for all we know.

While living with us, it was his job to chop the firewood, stack it, and bring it up to the house, which saved me the job for some time.

He was an avid reader of Zane Grey cowboy books and had a stack of them, but never offered to let us read them. One night while Mum was out, Barry, Percy, and I were sitting at the kitchen table with Percy reading one of his books. I don't know what Barry and I were doing, but to annoy Percy (which was my wont), while he was reading, I bounced a balloon up and down on the table. Percy disappeared for a while and returned to his book. I noticed that as I was bouncing the balloon, his hand was slowly getting closer to the balloon and had a pin held in it, which amused me greatly. When he got close to the balloon, I let the balloon down and left the table to spoil his fun.

The old bugger slept in the same sleepout as Barry and me, which was very cosy with only one small wardrobe to share and other stuff shoved under our beds. And because he only bathed when Mum got fed up with the smell of him, our room was always a bit 'high'.

Nana and Pop Howson

Nana Howson was Mum's mother, and was married to Grandad Forster (Percy) at the time Mum and her siblings were born. Percy didn't come home from the war, and nobody knew where he was so Nana was granted a divorce and married Frank Howson. Frank was a water meter reader for the Water Board until he retired.

When Percy eventually decided to show himself after the war, he was ropable that Nana had re-married and was going to murder Pop. Percy, armed with an axe, was about to clobber Pop while he was sleeping when he realised the bloke in the sleepout bed was his own son, and stopped himself in time.

As kids, we used to visit Nana and Pop when they lived in Douglas Avenue, South Perth, which was a treat for a few reasons, one being that Nana always gave us two bob to spend at the shop or the zoo. There was a small shop around the corner on Canning Highway that I loved, and I would buy musk penny sticks and liquorice straps. Liquorice straps were about 450mm long by about 25mm wide and delicious. We would go to the South Perth Zoo, which was close to their place, and what a disaster that was for the animals, with ridiculously small cages and compounds. The larger animals were zombie-like, rocking back and forth as they could hardly move around. There were rides to be had on an elephant which we never did – I assume because of the cost – a lovely old merry-go-round, and a miniature train, which we did get to ride on.

At the South Perth Zoo (Perth Zoological Gardens) C1955

Behind Nana and Pop's house, the bush went downhill to Mill Point Road, and we had a ball running around playing there. Unlike our bush at home, here it was just low-lying scrub, so vastly different from the timbers we were used to.

Nana and Pop sometimes visited us in Bunbury on their sidecar, with pop driving it and with nana in the sidecar. I thought that was unbelievably cool.

Pop's son, Bobby, had several motorbikes in a shed at the back of Nana and Pop's house, some of which he raced. I think he must have lived elsewhere because I only remember seeing him there once. Unfortunately, Bobby got killed on one of his road bikes when he overtook a mate on a bend and hit a car coming the other way.

Part Three

Primary School

I attended South Bunbury Primary School from 'Bubs' class to Grade Seven and then on to Bunbury Senior High School from there. My father and I were both in love with my first Primary School teacher, Miss Rooney, as she was a gorgeous blonde.

We kids all walked to school, five kilometres return, every day, rain, hail or shine, and with no shoes. Not many kids wore shoes in those days as money was always a problem so close to the end of the war.

In Grade Two, we had a teacher called Mrs Williams, and what a dragon she was. She wore glasses attached to a chain around her neck so she could take them off and not lose them. I've hated those glasses chains ever since and would never wear one, despite now seeing the sense in them.

One day, some mongrel kid had defecated all over the toilet floor and another kid and I were detailed off to clean it up. Why us I don't know, but it wasn't a pleasant experience.

When small and in the lower classrooms I didn't like using the toilets in the main part of the school because the bigger kids would be fighting and locking each other in the cubicles, so when the recess bell rang, I'd be the first out the door, racing over to a large tree in the yard for a wee. I didn't give a thought to the neighbours being able to see me, and I don't know if any of them ever did.

I must've been worried about not being allowed to go to the toilet for a wee, so asked Dad what I should do. His reply was: "Well, if the teacher won't let you go, just pull it out and piddle on the floor." *Big help.*

We had swimming lessons during school hours and were bussed to the Jetty Baths for them. We also had swimming races there, and the only style I ever did well in was backstroke, where I finished one race in second place.

In the early classes we used pencils to write. Then, as we got older, we used pens and ink. Each wooden desk had an ink well in the top right-hand corner and some kid got the job of filling the wells up each day. One day we were mucking around, and I hadn't seen the wells filled up, so picked one up and pretended to throw ink at a mate. Boy, did I get into trouble for that. My mate, Geoff Simmons, was covered in blue ink, and I was given the cane again.

I was good at getting into trouble by accident, as above. Another day I was playing with my *cap rocket*, which was a plastic rocket ship that had a head that screwed off so you could place a cap into it. You would screw the cap back on and throw it at the ground. The head had a metal rod sticking out of it that slammed back into the cap, exploding it when it hit the ground.

I always had to go one better than everybody else so I threw mine straight up with three caps in it so it would hit the ground harder and hopefully make a louder explosion.

Unfortunately for me, one of my girl classmates, Christine Kitchen, happened to walk into the landing zone and the rocket hit her on the arm. She had a white cardigan on, and the exploding cap sent out gunpowder ash and left powder burns on her cardigan arm.

She got all excited and went and dobbed me in for burning her cardigan – in the shit again!

In the later years, biros became available and we were allowed to use them. We had a new boy from over East join our class; he brought a red ink biro with him which was a marvel and wondrous thing to me, a stationery freak.

I had some favourite teachers I still remember, one of them was Mr Wroth, who taught us handy manual stuff, as well as our normal lessons. I made a knife sheath for my hunting knife and wore it with the knife in it everywhere I went, except school. Mr Wroth had the class make a large book about Bunbury with pictures and a plastic cover with some beach sand inside it, to send to a school somewhere in America.

A couple of times he read a story to us by Henry Lawson that really cracked us up. It was *The Loaded Dog*, a real icon of a story.

There was a Catholic School nearby where the teachers were all nuns and the kids had to wear uniforms. As was the norm in those days, there was bigotry in all spheres of life, and we didn't like the Catholic kids at all. Why? Dunno!

We had a song we'd sing about them; "Convent dogs, sitting on logs, eating maggots out of frogs."

I think Dad told us that he and his mates had sung the same song when they were kids.

But once again, we never got into trouble, either because the Convent kids didn't complain, or the nuns didn't care?

Other nice teachers I remember are Miss Turner, Mr

Benson, and Headmaster Mr Gasmeer. Mr Gasmeer always wore a suit and looked the real professional. He took a real interest in our class and gave us special tasks to complete because we were the top Year Seven class, and his pride and joy.

Mr Benson was a 'teaching Deputy' and was the person who the 'bad' boys were sent to to get the cane. He'd say: "Put your hand out, boy, and meet Jimmy" – the name of his cane. He would then give the kid 'six of the best' whacks across the fingers.

One smartarse kid used to pull his hand away just as the cane came down, so Mr Benson thought he'd trick him by aiming higher up the arm. But this time the kid didn't pull his hand back and got a whack across his wrist which made the wrist come up in an enormous lump and made him scream. I don't know who was more scared, the kid or Mr Benson.

There was a deli across the road from the school where we'd go during lunch break to buy lollies. Other boys would shoplift stuff from there so I thought, *I can do that,* so one day I pinched a packet of pea seeds. I didn't want them of course, so on the way back to school I opened the packet and spread the seeds on the ground.

Despite primary school being a bit of fun and having some nice teachers, by the end of my time there, I was over it, and couldn't wait to get out on my own.

High School

At Bunbury Senior High School (BSHS), we had to wear a uniform, including shoes, which I had to go without until Mum could afford them. When I acquired a uniform, it was all hand-me-downs from my cousins, but I was never offended by it as that was the way it was for a lot of the population so I accepted it without any fuss.

The BSHS is on top of the highest hill in Bunbury and we had to walk up what seemed like thousands of stairs from any direction. Climbing up that hill would bring on asthma attacks most days and, as we had to wear ties as part of our uniforms, I thought I was surely going to die before I got there. My mother took pity on me (probably the first and only time) and wrote a letter to the principal, asking if I could be excused from wearing a tie because of asthma. Amazingly, the Principal agreed, and I was the only kid at the school who didn't have to wear one.

I also suffered from hay fever although I had no idea I had a problem, and I was never taken to a doctor about it. I was constantly blowing my nose and went to high school with about seven hankies in my pockets and school case. At each break, I would hang my soaked hankies in my locker to dry and re-use, so effectively using more than the seven hankies during the day.

I hid my bike at Aunty Dora's house which was in Money Street, halfway up the hill, because even in those days, bikes would get pinched. I had a carrier over the rear wheel of my bike to carry my school case, which was made of some sort of brown fibreboard. I would polish the case each week with tan shoe polish, as it was special to me. They were expensive and one of the few things of value I had, and I still have it today. Mum may have bought it with money from one of the scholarships she managed to get for me.

Sometimes I would get a lift home for lunch with a friend, but Phillip's father always dropped us off late at the bottom of Boulters Heights, and Phillip would run up the hill – he was a runner in athletics and used it as training. I would be stressed out not being able to breathe, so took a long time to ascend the hill.

My favourite teachers at BSHS were Ron Clarke and David Black. David was the TV political commentator on Channel Two during elections.

Those of us who did metalwork had to get ourselves down to a metalwork annexe for the morning near where Jetty Road is now. There was a tearoom opposite, and we would go over there for our morning break to buy a cake or lollies. Once again, there was some shoplifting happening there and just as bad, some of us would pour salt into the sugar containers. What those shopkeepers had to put up with was crazy, but I guess not as crazy as what people do to them now.

Textbooks didn't change every year, as they do now, and, as most families were poor, the high school had a loan scheme to save families money. One book I borrowed was that old it had my cousin Glen's name written in it – he was nine years older than me, and I was gobsmacked at the amazing coincidence of us both having the same book.

For some years after the war, high schools had army cadets as part of their curriculum, where the boys who wanted to joined up and learned how to handle weapons and march etc, just like the real army. There were no girls in the cadets, woodworking, metalworking, or tech drawing, of course. They were only allowed to take part in cooking, sewing, and other domestic classes.

Incredibly the boys could take their army surplus supplied Enfield 303 rifles home with them, but I hoped and assumed without ammunition.

Part Four

Entertainment around Bunbury

I believe I was born into and grew up in the best era for seeing so many changes in life, living, housing, and technology of all types.

When I was ten years old, I witnessed the first man-made satellite orbiting the earth, launched in October 1957. It was made by the Russians and was called the *Sputnik*, which was a Russian word for spouse/travelling companion (or satellite when interpreted in an astronomical context.)

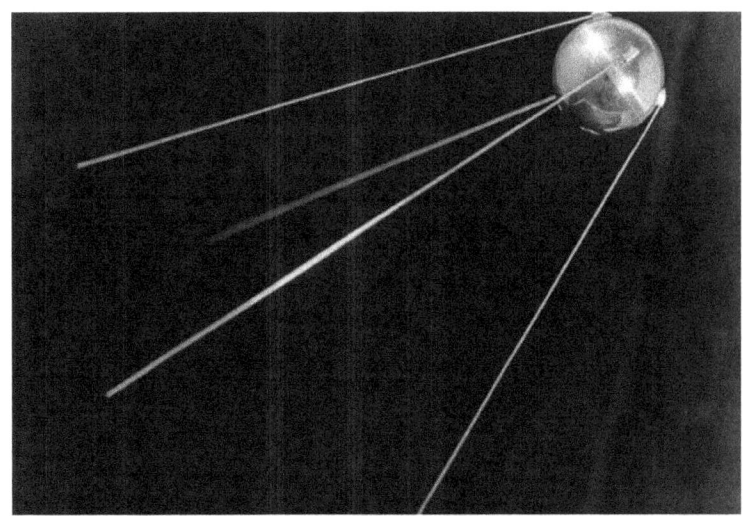

Sputnik

We would go outside to the road at the front of our house and watch the *Sputnik* race across the sky at 29,000 kilometres per hour. Or so we thought! *Sputnik* was too small to see with the naked eye. What we could see was the rocket that had propelled it and was following *Sputnik* in its orbit until the rocket fell away after some time.

We saw the last of the silent movies and enjoyed the new 'talkies', all in black and white. The naysayers, of course, said the talkies were only a fad, but like all new technology they went ahead in leaps and bounds into glorious colour too.

The movies then were all made inside large sheds and now if you watch them you cringe looking at the 'outdoor' props, poor acting, and feeble stunts.

We made our own wireless (radio) sets using a Germanium Diode and a set of ex-army headphones which worked well. Then we obtained a *real* wireless from somewhere that we could change stations on. This wireless body was made of Bakelite, the first plastic invented. We didn't know it at the time, but Bakelite is a deadly compound made from carbolic acid (phenol), formaldehyde, and asbestos, which, when cut or machined, leaves a deadly powder.

My cousin Loy had a wind-up gramophone we played heavy vinyl 78rpm records on and from there through the years, we went through small 45rpm records, large 33rpm records, cassette tapes, all the way up to DVDs and on. The old gramophones had small sharp needles that had to be replaced after only ten playings, and I'm sure wore out the records in a short time.

One night while at Glen's place, Loy's boyfriend Terry

(later to become her husband) walked in a bit flustered and asked Glen if he could help by towing Terry's bogged VW out of the dunes. Glen grabbed a length of rope and we all jumped in his ute and went up to the dunes overlooking the beach to find Loy sitting waiting for Terry's return. After some grunting and digging, we finally got the VW out and the lovers drove off into the dark.

Entertainment was a simple affair in the 50s, and far less technical than today. When TV first came to WA, people would go to town and watch TV through the window of Boans department store as they left their displays turned on for this purpose. Some people even took their chairs to set up on the footpath. We didn't get a TV set until well into the 1960s. Before that, if we wanted to watch a show, we'd visit friends who had a set. The reception in Bunbury was dismal with 'snow' on the screen, which these days we call *white noise*.

Before TV, we all sat around the wireless (radio) and listened to music and stories, some of which were serials spread over weeks. There were crime stories such as *The Concrete Jungle* and *CIB*, which were true crime stories played out. There was comedy shows too, such as *Yes Sir*, set in a classroom of dysfunctional kids, and *The Goon Show*, a classic comedy people still parody. Then there was *Pick-a-Box*, run by Bob and Dolly Dyer, a game show that went on to be a hit on early TV.

Mum knitted jumpers, gloves, and other clothing for us while singing to us as she had a fine voice and she sometimes sung at weddings and parties as well. Her favourite wedding song was *Ave Maria*, and some songs she sang to us while sitting around the fire at night were: *Old*

Shep and *Que Sera*.

Window shopping was a big thing too when we, and other people, would get dressed up and go looking in the shop windows after hours to see the new items and dream of owning them someday.

One of the few sports I played out of school was tennis, and we played on somebody's bitumen court near Beach Road on Saturday mornings. One day, some dopey woman came over to berate us for swearing loudly, and we didn't have a clue what she was on about. It turned out she could hear Barry calling somebody a buzzard when they hit a ball passed him, and she thought he was yelling "you bastard."

We used to walk down to the local football oval – now called Hands Memorial Oval – on Sundays to watch the footy and cheer on our team, South Bunbury Tigers. One of their best players those days was a mate of Dad's, Ron Buswell, who was short and stocky, but quick. His playing position was Rover, and he ran rings around other teams' players. I was reminded of Ron years later when Barry Cable was Rover for Perth in the WAFL.

While visiting the Nashes in Carlisle as a kid, we'd walk to the Archer Theatre (1.5 kilometres each way) on a Saturday afternoon to watch the flicks. It was after watching a cartoon there one day I came to realise that I had a macabre sense of humour. A *Goofy* cartoon showed him dodging a raging bull in a bullring and then hiding in a gap in the fence to get away from the bull. After a while, *Goofy* peeked out to see if the bull had gone and he couldn't see it anywhere so stepped out. The bull had been running so fast that *Goofy* couldn't see him and as he stepped out, the bull flattened him. I couldn't stop laughing and even laughed as

I thought about it on the walk back to Nash's place.

Going for a Sunday drive was a treat. We could end up anywhere for a picnic or some other fun activity. If the orchards had ripe fruit in them, Dad would stop the car where it couldn't be seen and help himself to a bag of oranges or apples or whatever else was on offer. He was even known to cut a length of fencing wire out of somebody's fence for when he needed some wire.

Mornington Mill was a place we visited a few times. I think it was there we found an old shack to explore. Inside were fantastic sketches of men in striped trousers, smart jackets, and top hats, which fascinated me. There were also some metalworking files which seemed a bit out of place.

When out with Dad in the car, just the two of us, if I spotted a pretty girl, I'd wolf whistle her then duck down, so he'd get the blame and a nasty glare.

Dad often went to the Picton Hotel for a couple of drinks during the 'session' at the end of a Sunday drive. Women weren't allowed in the bar in those days, so Mum would sit with us in the car and Dad would bring her a lemon squash and we kids a raspberry squash. This was a real treat for us, and I looked forward to it as the squash was delicious. Sometimes we'd end our drive with fish and chips and, while driving along, we'd hold our chips out the window of the car to cool them down. Other times we'd get an ice cream cone as a treat.

We had a song about one of the horse-riding young socialite ladies in the district, and one day we (Barry, Phillip Braund, and I) sung it out loud while she was on her horse prancing around the paddock nearby with her girlfriends on their horses.

"Glenice Smart did a fart and blew the baker off his cart." This, for some reason, annoyed her and she chased after us. Being the youngest and slowest, I was the only one she caught, and copped a whipping from her riding crop.

When there was a special event such as the Bunbury Show, teams of marching girls from all over the south-west came to town to march the streets and the oval during the show. Their uniforms were very colourful, and they wore large white gloves like motorcyclists' gauntlets.

There were also motorbike stuntmen, who rode their bikes around a large steel 'Ball of Death' cage. Sometimes there would be two bikes racing around in it at the same time.

There was also a boxing tent that people paid to go into to watch boxing. Blokes were invited to try themselves out against the boxers within the troupe, but I doubt if anybody beat them.

On Sundays, the Salvos brass band would walk around the streets and play their songs at various places. I was in awe of the beautiful shiny brass instruments they played and enjoyed the spectacle. We had no other live shows in Bunbury in those days that we kids were taken to, so, boring as it sounds, it was a treat to me. We were lucky enough to have the Salvos stop at our corner often, and we'd hang around nearby listening to their music.

I provided entertainment that amused and amazed all the kids in the neighbourhood: when Mum inserted suppositories in my anus as one of the treatments I went through to combat my asthma, I would be head down, bum up on my bed while Mum spread my cheeks and inserted them. There was no privacy in those days, and luckily, I didn't get embarrassed at all.

My parents must have gone away for a few days, and I spent those days with Uncle Clarrie and Aunty Joyce McManus. Uncle Clarrie (an ex-sailor) had to do the dirty deed with my suppositories, and I didn't even get embarrassed having him do it.

We diligently saved our money to buy fireworks: crackers, skyrockets, Catherine wheels, jumping jacks, and throwdowns, and the like, to let them off later in the year – on Guy Fawkes Night (5th of November.) Mr Wells, from the local corner shop, gave me a Kraft Cheddar Cheese box to store my valuable fireworks in until the night of firing them all off. The skyrockets were fired from a king brown beer bottle and the Catherine wheels were nailed to the fence.

Bonfires were built all over Bunbury and lit up on Bonfire Night, as it was also known, and great fun was had by all. Eventually, fireworks were banned in Australia due to idiots throwing crackers at and aiming skyrockets at people, causing catastrophic injuries.

Kids being kids, we used to blow up all sorts of things with our 'penny bombs' and later 'fourpenny bombs' which were a lot bigger and went off with a really loud bang. A penny bomb cost one penny, and the fourpenny bomb cost fourpence.

We used to catch gilgies in the creeks to cook and eat, but one day we decided to see what damage a fourpenny bomb could do to a gilgie. We put the biggest gilgie we caught on top of a fourpenny bomb, lit the fuse, and stepped back. When it went off and the smoke cleared, there was no sign of the gilgie at all.

One day on the Wendt farm, we bored a hole in an anthill with a stick and stuffed a penny bomb in the hole to see what damage we could do. The bomb didn't go off and as I bent down to see what was happening, it exploded, and I got covered in dirt and ants. Luckily, nothing went in my eyes.

I heard of other kids blowing up people's letterboxes or placing a penny bomb in the back hatch of an outdoor dunny while somebody was having a quiet sit. A shame I didn't think of that – it would've been great fun.

A lot of us had magnifying glasses which we used to closely look at stamps and other interesting stuff. We also of course, used them to start fires and burn ants – we were feral little buggers.

I have always loved the bush, and as kids we would spend all day out picking wildflowers, or just wandering around enjoying the ambience. We sometimes took some food or lollies with us and could stay out as long as we liked, providing we were home before dark. One favourite was to take some spuds and light a fire to cook them in; no aluminium foil then, we just chucked them in the fire and poked a stick into them to drag them out when we thought they were cooked.

We also played for hours in the sandhills at the end of Halsey Street, where the sand was excavated and carted away to who-knows-where. Originally a bulldozer was used to push the sand up a 'chinaman' ramp, off the end down into a truck. Around the late 1950s, they started using a front-end loader as they were more efficient.

Chinaman during WWII (not in Bunbury)

One day, a mate and I were sitting on the edge of a sand cliff above the loader watching it take the sand away from below us. I felt the earth move suddenly, so immediately shuffled backward only to see my mate disappear with a large portion of the hill down toward the loader, a drop of about twenty metres. When I looked over the edge, I saw him bolting out toward the road. I don't know who got the biggest shock – him, or the loader driver – but it was good to watch.

A special part of our entertainment started near the foot of the Bunbury jetty and years later moved to Guppy Park at the end of Victoria Street. This was the Penny Arcade, which also had a merry-go-round. With just a penny, we could win a packet of Wrigley's chewing gum or a packet of *Lifesavers* from what now look like one-arm bandits. The arcade disappeared years ago, but the machines are still owned by the same family, and some are still used along with other more modern machines at shows around WA.

Interestingly, Barry's grandson Jordan has worked with them in a part-time position.

At the suburb of Bunbury, now known as Marlston, was an enormous shed that stored wheat while waiting for a wheat ship to take it away. Because of the large sand drifts, the roof of the shed met the sand and we used to walk up the sand and all over the roof. Oddly enough, we didn't get into trouble for that; everybody was more laid back than today.

We made some pocket money by collecting beer, cooldrink, and milk bottles and returning them. The beer bottles were picked up by the 'Bottle-O' – more correctly named the 'Marine Dealer' – in crates that held thirty-six bottles. We were paid a halfpenny for each bottle. Empty beer bottles were called 'dead marines' when I was a kid, and I guess they got that name from the title Marine Dealer. The cooldrink bottles were worth more but the milk bottles brought a real bonus at sixpence each.

My Uncle Clarrie Forster over the road had at least one horse. I sometimes accompanied him on his horse-drawn dray out to the bush to collect firewood. I couldn't get enough of the bush, and it was good to wag school.

My cousin Pat McManus used to go out the end of Minninup Road into the bush (which is now all houses,) and catch brumbies. He kept and trained them in a paddock just up the road from our place. They were great to watch: beautiful beasts running past us proudly with their heads held high while we were outside the fence admiring them. I had a few rides on his and other horses but was put off horses forever when, one day, while visiting Grandad Britza in hospital, a young girl was wheeled in with blood all over her face after a horse had kicked her.

I had a couple of nicknames for a while; the longest-lasting was *Jacko*, as according to the kid who christened me with it, I laughed like a kookaburra. At the time, kookaburras were also called Jackos. The other nickname was *Mighty Mouse,* which a kid dubbed me when we were racing our pushbikes around a dirt track in Forrest Park. There was a jump as part of the track, and I could fly further than anybody else off that jump. This kid yelled out as I was approaching it: "Look out! Here comes Mighty Mouse!" and it stuck for a while.

There was a drain – called Five Mile Brook by some – that was built to drain water from a swamp, where the suburb Dalyellup is now. It wound its way to the ocean at the end of Hayward Street. That area was known as 'Punchbowl' and had a dressing room for swimmers nearby. I think there may have been a shop there too, and later a caravan park behind the hill near the junction of Hayward Street and Holywell Street.

Where the drain crossed Minninup Road and Clarke Street, the road was raised sharply over the drain and sharply down again. One day I saw an older mate and motocross racer, George Webber on his motorbike use the rise on Clarke Street as a jump, which greatly impressed me. I never tried it because I never rode motorbikes on the road, but boy, it looked like a heap of fun.

We caught many gilgies in the drain; at first, using meat tied to a string and when the gilgies grabbed the meat, we'd slowly drag it in and use a kitchen strainer to scoop up the gilgie. Later, Dad made us small drop nets like crabbing drop nets to make it easier to catch them.

I joined the Cubs (part of the Scouting organisation) for a short while where we were taught knot tying and other life skills that were not that interesting to me. The straw that broke the camel's back for me was one evening I got a piece of fine rubber in my eye. This was very painful and the rubber stayed there until I got home and Mum removed it, so I never went back. The material was finely chopped up rubber spread on the floor to make it softer to play and fall on.

I also joined the Police Boys Club, which entailed more sporting activities that suited me better, was more fun and I stayed there longer. One of the activities was boxing which I excelled in until one boy connected with my face and I thought: *Bloody hell, that hurts*, so I gave that up for other less painful pursuits.

One Christmas, when I was about 5, I received a box of great stuff, including a ball of string which I thought was the best thing ever. And so started my love affair with all things stationery.

We made our own Christmas decorations in those days including chains made from crepe paper, hung across the kitchen and lounge room ceilings.

I was always a bit of a rebel which got me into a bit of trouble and may be the reason Mum always said: "Robert's a bugger of a kid," and added, "I don't know any kid named Robert, that's not a bugger of a kid." I thought this was a bit harsh but it pleased me at the same time.

When we got our first telephone, I heard that if you rang a certain number, the phone would ring itself as a check to see if it was operating properly. I'd often ring that number and jump into the lounge room to hide while Mum answered it and swore because nobody was on the other end. That cracked me up, and I had to make sure I didn't laugh out loud, or I wouldn't be here to tell the story.

A trick Dad taught us was tying a purse to a length of thin fishing line and placing the purse on the edge of the road. Then we hid behind a bush holding the other end of the line. When somebody tried to pick it up, we'd yank the purse away and get a thrill out of their response. We caught lots of victims – people stopping their cars, and walkers bending over to pick it up. A kid from up the road tried to pick it up but it jumped back several inches away from his hand, so he tried again with the same result. After the second attempt, he screamed and ran up the road bawling, which left us howling with laughter.

During January, the year after Dad died, I attended the Legacy Camp at Busselton with a bunch of other boys who were sons of deceased ex-servicemen. The camp was run by members of the SAS who were a great bunch of blokes. They taught us all manner of things, including how to make our beds properly. We had to help make our breakfast, and the way they did the toast was far different from how we did it. They had a baking dish with butter melted in it and when the bread was toasted, we used a shaving brush dipped into the butter to wipe it over the bread.

We were taken on bus trips to various places, including Yallingup Beach. I was nearly fourteen years old and still a superhero and had heard there was excellent surf at Yallingup. I body-surfed at Bunbury with the biggest waves I could catch, and thought I could do the same at Yallingup on the waves that were a couple of hundred metres offshore. They didn't look too big from the shore, but brother, when you're close and looking way up at them, they are scary, so I turned around and swam back to shore.

During one of these trips, we stopped at a roadside shop for drinks and lollies. One of the other kids bought a packet of Cheese Twisties and shared them with me. I was amazed at the fantastic taste and became addicted to them, and have spent the rest of my life introducing them to my kids, grandkids, and anybody else I think needs a treat.

The SAS blokes taught us to play baseball and, being my first time, when I hit the ball and dropped the bat, it slipped and went flying backward hitting one of the other kids on the chin, knocking him unconscious.

Opposite the Parade Hotel on the other side of the river, was a large muddy area with trees, low shrubbery and mangroves (furtherest south in Australia) which became known as *The Blunders*. Many years ago, a bloke named Paddy decided to keep his pigs on an island there, but the pigs had other ideas and took off across the river. Unfortunately, the pigs drowned, and the area was nicknamed *Paddy's Blunder*, which in the Australian way got shortened to just *The Blunders*.

In 1954 a group of blokes, including a friend of our family, Colin Resta, got together and decided the Blunders would be a great place to hold mud scrambles in their cars. They had a variety of old jalopies they modified by removing body parts to lighten them. Then they fitted snow chains to the tyres to give them traction in the mud. Originally, they didn't have roll cages fitted as safety wasn't thought about much in those gung-ho days. After a couple of years though, they saw sense and fitted the cages.

One day while watching the action with Dad on a high

part near the road, people started yelling and running for some reason. Suddenly the reason became apparent as a tiger snake slid passed us. Dad grabbed a piece of fencing wire or similar and beat the beast to death, much to everybody's relief.

The Blunders was another place we used to go crabbing as young kids, with Dad and Uncle Ted. Being under water for a lot of the year, and wet the rest of the time, there were plenty of mozzies to keep our hands busy.

I took the photos below with my Kodak Brownie box camera.

Colin Resta

Colin Resta in his ute and another vehicle come together

Colin Resta flying through the mud

Around the Houses Road Racing

Bunbury was one of the towns in the Southwest that held 'around-the-houses' road racing, which was a big hit with residents and visitors alike. Many circuits were laid out over the years that took in many of the streets in and around the town centre, Glen Iris, and Vittoria.

1963 may have been the last time they held the races within the CBD as an Australian rider, Kel Karuthers, who would become the World Champion in 1969, brought his four-cylinder Honda 250cc bike to Bunbury to race. Fantastic for us, but not for the hospital patients and non-motorcycle fans living in the middle of the circuit – that bike had the loudest howl ever to be heard in Bunbury – it was awesome.

When racing on public roads, the power/light poles had hay bales stacked up against them to protect any rider unlucky enough to hit one. One street used in an event (Symmons Street) went directly west toward the ocean and did a 90-degree left turn just before the ocean into Ocean Drive. On that bend were several 'silent policemen' in the middle of the road for the racers to avoid, which looked a bit dangerous to me. The silent policemen were about 2-3 metres tall with a base of about a metre square, and as far as I know, no rider ever hit one.

Race cars also competed on public roads. One year there was a Ferrari racing car, which was really special. I would've only been about nine years old and was with Barry watching these races when he decided to get a photo of the Ferrari with his Brownie Box camera. This is fine if you know what you're doing, but he aimed his camera across the road and hit the shutter as the red beast flew passed. Of course, he only got a photo of the people on the other side of the road.

Bunbury Shops

Some of the shops in Bunbury included The *Du Drop In* tearooms where, when shopping with Mum, we'd have a banana split or strawberry frappe; *Cronshaws*, a clothing shop; *Thomas Chemist*, where I got my films developed, as they were the only shop in Bunbury to do their own developing – all other pharmacies sent the film to Perth to be developed. *Boulters Menswear* was the 'in' place for gents to buy their clothes. A family friend of ours, Bob Braund, was the manager there. *Bon Marche was* a clothing shop for all, where I did my clothes shopping and, because money was tight, they let me have the clothes on "appro" and I paid them off. There was a *Woollies*, of course (didn't every town have a Woolies?) and *Coles*, where, when you entered, there was a double counter stretching out in front of you with attendants in between and a counter down each side of the shop with attendants behind each one. *Caris Brothers* was a jewellery shop; *Ezi Walkin*, a shoe shop; *South's*, a furniture shop and *Gee Dees*, an electrical shop. It was named *Gee Dees* because the owners were Mr Godley and Mr Davies.

Outside Cronshaws was where I had my first prang on my crutches while recovering from my motocross injuries. It was raining, and so, being clever, I decided to travel close to the shop windows where there wasn't so much water. Unfortunately, being an area of little foot traffic, when wet it was slippery as ice, and I went arse up. A lady picked up my crutches and tried to help me up, but I managed on my own. The second crutches prang I had was at the motocross track near where I sustained all my injuries. I simply tripped over something I didn't see.

When I was about four or five years old, Barry and I used to ride our little tricycles to Gibson's butcher shop to buy meats for the family. The shop was in Constitution Street, about a 1.5 kilometres return trip.

On the corner of Minninup Road and Constitution Street, there was a horse trough with water in it for people to water their horses as they rode around Bunbury. There were horse troughs all around Bunbury for the same reason. The many horses on the streets in those days were a bonus for keen gardeners. They kept an eye on the roads when hearing a horse go by and were glad to clean up the horses' dung to put on their vegetable and flower gardens – there was no commercial fertilizers in those days.

As housing spread south passed our house, a corner shop was built and run by Mr Wells, a bloke who was friendly and kind to us kids. I sometimes went there to buy Mum's cigarettes for her, which now is illegal for kids to do. That shop is where I saw my first plastic bags, a wonder after paper bags! It even had printing on it: *Lanchoo Tea*. One of my favourite lollies were *Chocos*, a precursor to *Smarties* with different colours, but *Chocos* were shaped like an orb. They were four-a-penny, which meant you got four for the cost of a penny (one cent.) When I bought a shillings worth or more Mr wells would chuck in several extras.

A butcher shop was also eventually built nearby. The Butcher made his own polony, which was delicious with a nice texture, far better than the factory produced polony.

We used to bundle up newspapers the family had finished reading and sell them to this butcher for wrapping up the meat as he sold it. He had an enormous log standing in the middle of the shop work area on which he chopped the meat up. The floor of the shop was covered in sawdust, I assume to soak up any spilled blood from butchering the carcasses. I was spellbound by the butcher wrapping up the meat when he pulled down a length of string from where it was hanging from the ceiling. He had a method of winding it around fingers on both hands, pulling it, and breaking it with apparent ease. I tried this for ages without success and got frustrated with my failure and nearly tearing another finger off.

Daredevil

We did a lot of swimming at Koombana Bay where there was a jetty for fishing and diving off. One day I ran to the end and jumped off without looking to see if it was safe, and there below was another boy swimming. I landed on him and was immediately in pain with a torn ligament. I slowly swam to shore, limped to my bike and rode it home with only one leg pushing a pedal. I was on crutches for ages before it healed. Months later I thought to myself, "I wonder if that other kid got hurt."

We often visited friends – Bill and May Edwards – in Collie. One day a gang of us kids was running up against and bouncing off their full-height hedge across the front of their property. Being the superhero, I climbed on top of the side fence and launched myself off the fence onto the top of the hedge for an impressive super bounce.

Unfortunately, the hedge had just been trimmed, and a sharp stick stuck into my bum. I walked into the house with blood running down my legs. Mum was used to me being injured and bleeding a lot by now, so she just cleaned me up while laughing at some of the other women's comments that I didn't understand. It was off to the Collie hospital for stitches then a couple of weeks of using cut-up rags to wipe my bum and very painful defecating.

May Edwards was nicknamed 'Collie May' because we already had relations and friends named May. Her husband Bill was a shit-head and would often bash May up. His only redeeming point (in my opinion) was, he was a maniac driver. We were going over the Collie Bridge with Bill driving when there were a couple of fishermen on the edge of the bridge fishing in the Collie River below. The bridge was entirely made of timber and had transverse timbers with two longitudinal rows of timbers leading over the bridge for the wheels to ride on. When we got close to the fishermen, Bill swerved at them to scare them – what a legend. I didn't have driving lessons at all, just did the test because I closely observed how people drove as I had some great drivers to learn from, including Bill.

Mind you, when I did my driving test, I stuffed a few things up. In the main street of Bunbury, after stopping, I 'kangaroo-hopped' up the street for a while with Barry laughing in his parked car watching. Luckily, I didn't see him there or I may have been more flustered than I already was. Also, in the main street, as we approached a crosswalk, a bloke on the other side of the road stepped onto the crosswalk. I put my foot down to beat him and the Cop said, "You should've stopped for him," to which I responded, "But I got there first."

We had to do a hill start from first gear and a handbrake stop, but I forgot to put the car back into first gear and stalled it the first time I tried. On the way back to the Police Station, there's a ninety-degree turn in the road with a 35mph speed limit which I took at 40mph. Amazingly, when we got back into the Station, the Cop said: "You made a couple of mistakes, but I can see you know how to control a car," and gave me my licence. I think he was scared I'd come back again if he failed me, and he may not survive my driving a second time.

Years later I was in Collie again with the Bunbury Motorcycle Club for a motocross event alongside Minninup Pool, Collie's 'swimming pool' in the Collie River. At lunchtime, we went to the pool for a cool-off and lunch, when the superhero in me came out again. I did a 'bombie' off the side of the diving board to splash one of my mates and his family sitting on the edge of the pool. Wouldn't you know it, as I straightened my legs out to re-surface, my feet dragged along the bottom of the river, and one foot was opened up by broken glass there. Off to the Collie hospital again for more stitches.

When the land was cleared for housing in the 50s, the trees were bulldozed up into long lines called windrows and then burnt. While they burned, we would collect offcuts of asbestos sheeting from building sites and chuck them in the fire to hear them explode. Great fun.

While staying at Uncle Ron and Aunty Shirley's place I was playing next door with Harry Butler's kids, climbing a big tree. The superhero came out in me again and, like Tarzan, leapt from one branch to another but my hands couldn't hold me up and I slipped to the ground landing on my bum. Yet another time I momentarily paralysed myself and was unable to stand up for a few minutes.

Barry and I were playing Cowboys and Indians one day and I was about two metres up a tree when he 'shot' me. Just like in the movies, I threw my hands up and fell out of the tree, conned again. It bloody hurt and I couldn't walk again for a few minutes.

Aunties and Uncles

The Forsters
(Mum's Grandmother and Uncles)

Diagonally opposite our house across the intersection lived my maternal great-grandmother. Behind this weatherboard house, which still exists, was a block of several acres. It had dozens of different fruit trees, vines, legumes, and bulbs. If it would grow in the Bunbury area, it was grown in this orchard.

I took all these fresh fruit and vegetables for granted and picked what I wanted when I wanted it. I had no idea how lucky I was to have this smorgasbord of fruit and vegetables to pick. There were different varieties of plums, figs, grapes, almonds, pears, and so on – marvellous – all kept under control by my mother's uncles, Clarry and George. That spoiled me and when I went to Perth to live, I couldn't bring myself to eat fruit that came from a shop – it just didn't feel right. I still don't eat a lot of fruit and vegies to this day.

There was a massive Mulberry tree in one corner of their orchard. It was easy to climb and had millions of mulberries on it every year. We all ate our fill from that tree and fought in it by throwing ripe mulberries at each other. We all went home with purple hands, faces, feet, and clothes, for which we were growled at, of course, but that didn't stop us from doing it again. Many of our cousins joined in the fighting, including Janice and Barbara Nash, who both remember the orchard and mulberry fights with fondness.

The orchard has now been replaced by a complex of housing units called *Forster Mews* after Nana Forster and her family.

Nana Forster must've died when I was young as I can't remember that happening. She was a lovely old lady who slept in the front bedroom in the northeast corner of the house. She had a large bed that was remarkably high off the floor for me, and hard to climb onto, but when we did, it was worth it. She had jars of hard-boiled lollies (including humbugs) on a shelf above her bed, and she always gave us some to eat.

Uncles Clarrie and George lived there until they died, and only ever rode pushbikes around Bunbury, as neither of them ever had a car. Uncle George was a chronic asthmatic, and on occasion, he'd crawl across the road and knock on our front door so Mum could take him to the hospital. He was also an avid bowler and rode his pushbike to the Bunbury Bowling Club on Forrest Avenue.

One of their sheds had their horse tack in it, including a horse collar and a light hame for fixing to the horse and attaching to the cart the horse would pull. We ended up with the hame, which was made of steel, on our patio. The photo shows one similar but looks like it's made from timber and leather.

Horse collar

Light hame

Uncle Clarrie used a scythe to cut the long grass on their block for decades. I don't think he ever bought a lawnmower, which means he would have used the scythe until he died in his 80s.

Scythe

The Forster Homestead in 2015

The Forster brothers were extremely frugal, to the point of manually cycling their new electric fridge on and off to save power, and didn't turn their lights on in the house at night. Their power bill showed they paid more for the supply charge than they did for the power they used, and that was in the early days of the supply charge when it was only about $6. The furniture never got moved, so they always knew where they were in the house and didn't need lighting to find their way around.

One day Mum went over for a visit and Uncle Clarrie was cooking something on the stove in a jam tin and using pliers to pick the tin up by its lid off the stove. They never owned a washing machine but used the old glass and timber washboard in the image below. A corner of the glass got broken, so they fashioned a piece of wood to replace it, and that has been well worn with years of use. The washboard is now on our patio wall alongside an old bellows that came from their place too.

Washboard and bellows

Uncle Pat and Aunty Judy Forster

I often wagged school to go with my Uncle Pat Forster (Mum's brother,) while he travelled around the south-west carrying out artificial insemination of cows. He told me that when they trained for this, they didn't wear a long glove up their arm as he did now but had to use a bare hand and arm. They needed to get a good feeling of the syringe while directing it into the right position inside the cow and while doing this, their hand and arm would get a green tinge from the cow dung. That hand went up the anus while the syringe went up the vagina.

Uncle Pat with his arm up a cow

I took the photo on the previous page with my Kodak Brownie box camera at Green's dairy on North Boyanup Road at Boyanup. I couldn't use the clip-on flash or the cow would've jumped and probably broken Uncle Pat's arm.

When Uncle Pat got to our place, he'd get under the dashboard of the government-issued car and disconnect the speedo, so management wouldn't know he'd detoured from his designated journey.

Uncle Pat and Aunty Judy had a shotgun wedding because Judy was pregnant at fifteen, and they went on to have five kids before she turned twenty-one. The last pregnancy was twins, so it's not as bad as it sounds.

I also wagged school to go with Uncle Don when he was felling trees around Noggerup for a local mill. He and a workmate felled an enormous jarrah tree using a large, two-man chainsaw and then 'de-barked' the tree with axes. This had to be done so the trees would be clean when delivered to the timber mill. This sometimes left a large slither of splinters where the axe went too deep. I was running along the de-barked tree with bare feet and, as I jumped off, my foot slid around the tree trunk and some large splinters went under the nail of a big toe. My toenail was ripped off and bits of splinter embedded in the meat of my toe, where they stayed for some months. Given there was no doctor or hospital in the bush, the wound was just wrapped up and I got on with life. A few months later, the festering toe ejected the last bits of wood and a new nail grew back, but only half of it took to the flesh. Now my nail is ugly with one-half pink, and the other dark.

Uncle George and Aunty Betty

Uncle George (Dad's older brother) built a speedboat and named it *Garlo*, a combination of his youngest kids' names (Garry and Loy). We had a ball riding in the front of the boat and, when we were going flat out, we bounced until our teeth nearly shattered as there were no seatbelts or cushions in speedboats. The speedboat races were held between the jetty and the jetty baths out into the harbour. All the boats those days were single-hulled and went amazingly fast considering the old grey Holden motors they had in them.

Uncle George worked on the Bunbury jetty and like a lot of the 'Lumpers' there rode his BSA Bantam motorbike to work out on the jetty. One day, he was giving a workmate a lift on the back of his bike, the mate carrying something across his back which Uncle George had forgotten about. As they attempted to pass a train on the jetty, whatever was on his mate's back, hit the train and overbalanced them, making them and the bike fall over the side of the jetty into the water. Uncle George lost the hearing in one ear when he hit the water, and his bike was never seen again. Both men were rescued and had no other physical injuries.

Uncle George and Dad used to sometimes talk in 'Pig Latin' where they took the first letter off a word, put it at the back of the word, and added 'ay'. For example, my name would be Obertray Ritzabay, and they were good at conducting a conversation like this. Unfortunately, it was awfully hard to understand what they were saying as they carried on a conversation.

Aunty Lorna (Mum's sister) and Uncle George

The Orrs were a fantastic aunty and uncle to me as well. George had a wicked sense of humour and Lorna was always kind to us. The following anecdotes are snippets from Auntie Lorna (Mum's baby sister and only nine years older than me.)

At Christmas, the women cooked up heaps of great food and the men did the cleaning up. Then on New Year's Eve, there was always a party with a keg of beer and, just before midnight, everybody piled into the cars and drove to Victoria Street in the middle of Bunbury. Hundreds of people gathered to see the new year in, celebrating on the road that was closed to traffic around the Rose Hotel. After all the cheering, throwing streamers, and kissing, they drove back to our house to finish off the keg and keep partying.

Mum had a hearing problem and wouldn't hear a baby (I assume Barry) calling for a feed during the night, so Dad would get up, change the baby's nappy, and put the baby on Mum's breast. He would then take the baby off the breast, bring up its wind and put it on the other breast, and repeat the operation, all while Mum was sleeping. This story by Aunty Lorna sounds to me very unlikely, as I can't see any mother sleeping through all that. But hey, who knows?

More from Aunty Lorna: Dad would get up in the mornings, get his breakfast and breakfast for Barry and me while we were still in bed and he'd go off to work as we ate our breakfast.

Aunty Hazel (Mum's sister) and Uncle Ted

Christmas school holidays were looked forward to for many reasons, one being some of our aunties, uncles, and cousins would come to Bunbury and stay in tents at the Baths or the Koombana Park Caravan Park. Uncle Ted and Aunty Hazel would stay at Koombana Bay and Uncle Teddy always brought his small boat with its British Seagull outboard motor, which he took us fishing in.

He caught Barry and me walking along the beach one day, breaking all the discarded bottles with rocks, and made us pick up all the broken glass and put it in a bin.

During my apprenticeship with Chamberlain Industries about a kilometre away, I lived with them, sleeping on the back verandah in a very tired old bed that sunk in the middle. While living at Aunty Hazel and Uncle Ted's place, I had my left shoulder surgically re-constructed and, when off work recovering, was riding my pushbike around including going over jumps with only one hand on the handlebars. I couldn't stand being bored and was lucky I didn't have a prang, or my surgery would've been wrecked, I'm sure.

Uncle Ted was a character. While living with them, if I had to get up early, he'd come out and say, "Wakey, wakey, hand off snakey."

Uncle Bill and Aunty May (no relation)

Uncle Bill and Aunty May, with their kids, stayed at the camping area along the beach at the Baths, and we played with those kids as well. No Engels in those days: they had a 'Coolgardie Safe' to keep their food cool. A Coolgardie Safe has metal wire sides with a timber or metal frame and a door covered in hessian with a water tray on the top. An end of the hessian was kept in the tray, feeding water down through it and the moving air kept the hessian and the food on shelves inside cool. There was another metal tray underneath it to catch any excess water from the hessian.

Aunty May (Mum's Aunty) and Uncle Bill

Aunty May McManus and her husband Bill, in my eyes, were very mean-spirited people who only ever scowled and growled. It's no wonder three of their four sons left Bunbury for Canberra, never to return except for the occasional holiday. All of them, Charlie, Clarrie, Billie, and Pat were fantastic people who were kind to everybody. I think my mother was in love with Charlie as she tended to swoon over him.

Pat was Barry's age and hung around our place a lot. He had a real flash pushbike with lots of lights – including indicators – which he was proud of. I was envious of this work of art.

May was sister to Mum's Dad Percy Forster. Lornes O'Brien was another sister.

Uncle Jack and Aunty Vi (Mum's first cousin Vi)

Another farm we frequented was Jack and Vi Gibson's farm at Burekup, another great adventure playground. Uncle Jack grew watermelons, corn, loquats, and other crops I can't remember. They had a large wagon wheel set horizontally on an axle for the kids to spin around on and, their large shed contained a mountain of hay bales. I guess they must have had cattle to need all that hay.

Aunty Vi always had a fresh cake or two, ready for visitors, so it was a great double whammy going to their farm.

Uncle Jack sometimes stopped at our place with his ute filled with watermelons – the round variety – on his way to a market or somewhere. While he was there, we were allowed to sell a couple of them on the side of the road as we ate our fill. I never saw the elongated watermelons until I moved to Perth.

Almost all our parents' friends were called Uncle or Aunty by us kids, so we didn't know who our 'real' Aunties and Uncles were.

Uncle Don and Auntie Dot (no relation)

The farm we spent the most time on was near Collie, jointly owned and operated by brothers Don and Alex Wendt. They both had houses on the farm about 200 metres apart. There was no power supply, so they had a generator and a large bank of batteries. I assume all their appliances were 12 volts or powered by kerosene, as many fridges were in those days.

There was an old BSA motorbike in a shed with a large crack through its crankcase though it was still rideable. Barry and his mate Phillip Braund would take the bike out and ride it, unpowered, and in neutral down a hill for fun, but I'm sure it was no fun pushing it back up the hill again. Looking back, I'm surprised Barry didn't order me to help push it back up the hill with them.

Nearby in the bush was an abandoned mica mine that still had an open almost horizontal shaft we could walk into. Despite being only around eleven years old, I could see that it wasn't safe as the timber was rotting so I stayed out of it. Barry and the older kids all explored it and survived. Maybe it was my claustrophobia or fear of the dark that stopped me, but I prefer to think it was my common sense.

There was a paddock with a crop growing in it and roos were getting into it at night. They couldn't all be shot, and nobody was going to sit out in the dark and cold waiting to shoot them anyway. The next best thing was to make snares out of fencing wire tied to the lowest wire of the fence at the spots where the roos came under the fence. This was easy, as the roos wore a well-defined track in the undergrowth as they headed to the fence. They always came in at speed, so as their head went through and their shoulders hit the snare, it would tighten up like a hangman's noose and strangle them. Sometimes, joeys would fall out of the struggling mothers' pouches and be left to die – a very cruel and now illegal way to cull roos.

They ran cattle on the farm and one day Don and Dad had a cow tied by its neck to a fence while they tugged a stillborn calf out of the cow. It took ages and they had fencing wire through the dead calf's eyes so they could have something solid to pull. Eventually, they succeeded in getting the calf out and the poor mother cow survived despite the stress and pain.

They had a small pine tree plantation on the property and some fruit trees, including a massive walnut tree alongside the house and persimmon trees nearby which the Currawongs loved to eat.

The house had a verandah around it. Inside, the light switches were on the ceiling with a string hanging down to pull when you wanted the lights on or off. As a kid, I was enthralled with these light switches and, when we had a large patio built at the back of our house in Safety Bay, we had those switches connected to our patio lights.

The 'Redex Reliability Trial' went through the area only a couple of kilometres from the Wendt farm so we went to watch the cars go through during the night. The trial travelled 16,900 kilometres from Sydney around Australia and back to Sydney and was won by a VW 1200 that year. That was a great experience for an eight-year-old, staying up late and having a large fire while we watched the cars go passed as fast as they could go.

Uncle George and Auntie Norrie (no relation)

George and Norrie Barker were family friends who lived at Gelorup in a tiny cottage with four kids but later built a larger house on the property as the family outgrew the cottage. Norrie was a prolific swearer and was known to us as the 'lady who swears'.

George was a full-time fireman at the Bunbury Fire Brigade, and he used to cut blokes' hair at the station in his spare time. I bought my own manual clippers and would take them to the station when I needed a haircut. George was a real character, full of interesting stories and anecdotes.

While in the bush on Barker's property, we made what we called kangaroo gings out of car tubes tied to the fork of a tree, and shot half house bricks through the bush at each other. You could hear the bricks flying through the tree twigs and leaves, and how nobody ever got hurt is beyond me now.

While our parents were inside with the Barkers, we'd take our gings out for a walk and shoot all the bottles that were discarded on the side of the road and the hubcaps of cars going passed on the Bussell Highway.

Our gings were part of our persona and went almost everywhere with us. I hung mine over my shoulder like a bandit's ammo belt and carried my ammo (rocks) in a bag Mum made for me, on a belt around my waist so I was always ready for action. We had a lot of fun annoying people by shooting rocks onto their corrugated iron roofs. The rocks landed with a loud bang and rattled down the roof. A lot of abuse come our way over this lark, but nobody knew who it was as we hid very well.

Birds were fair game but hard to hit, and when we did hit one and kill it, we'd cut a notch in the ging's prong like a gunslinger did with the butt of his sixgun – bragging rights. And of course, streetlights were an easy target as they didn't move.

Mr and Mrs Staley (no relation)

We used to spend a lot of time at Staley's farm in Ludlow which was a great adventure as they had enormous pigs and some cattle. Mrs Staley always had cakes for us and made me a pat of butter from the fresh milk their cows produced. Mr Staley had a magnificent white moustache, which was stained orange in the centre by the nicotine in the smoke from his pipe he sucked on.

They had a large, hand-cranked, white grinding wheel in the yard on which Mr Staley sharpened his axe and other farm tools. The wheel would've been about 750mm in diameter by about 100mm wide.

Their farm was called *Ambergate*, and they had a steel gate at the entry into the farm with letters spelling out the name. There is a Reserve nearby with heaps of wildflowers on it called Ambergate Reserve near Busselton where Chris and I have been a couple of times to enjoy the wildflowers. Coincidentally, Chris and I lived in Ambergate Close in Canning Vale for five years.

Cousins

We had lots of cousins from both our parents. Mum was one of seven children and Dad was one of four. All their siblings had multiple kids. We also had 'cousins' that were kids of our pseudo aunties and uncles.

Graeme Kenny

I knocked around with Graeme a lot, as he was the same age as me and also lived in Bunbury. We spent our summers on the beach, mainly at Hungry Hollow, where we body-surfed and fooled around on tractor tubes in the surf. It was great fun putting ourselves in a position to be dumped with no thought of hitting the bottom and getting hurt. Graeme and I were incredibly competitive with one another, always trying to outdo each other.

One day while waiting for Graeme to turn up at *Foamy Channel*, I was watching for him and when I saw him approach, I turned around and dived off the rocks into the sea. Like most teenagers, I didn't check to see where the water was at that stage and landed on my head in about 50mm of water. Luckily, I survived with just a very sore neck for a few weeks and, of course, never told Mum as I knew I would only get abused for being stupid. There's no compassion in our house, remember?

The rocks around Foamy Channel are black volcanic rocks with vertical faces the waves crash into. We body-surfed at the rocks and timed it exactly right, so the backwash halted our rush and pushed us back from the rocks in the nick of time. As another challenge, I dared Graeme to body-surf with me up the Foamy Channel which has a bend in it and the waves bounce from side to side. We had plenty of spectators for a while, then some of the gamer ones joined us in the fun.

Graeme bought a Vespa just after I had my racing accident, and when he picked me up for a ride, he didn't want to let me wear my new crash helmet because he said they were not needed with him riding. My life had just been saved by my helmet while racing, so I knew the benefits of them and eventually talked him into taking me for a ride with my helmet on.

Brian Kenny

Graeme's older brother, Brian (nickname Goofy as a kid and into his teens) sucked one of his fingers with the whole thing in his mouth. He couldn't be broken of this habit and eventually created a dent in the roof of his mouth and a deformed finger.

Brian bought himself a Ford Prefect which we all used to hoon around town in. One day, while hooning around dirt tracks near the Bunbury motocross track, I hung my body out of the window pretending to be a sidecar passenger keeping the car upright. I would've been dead or crippled if the car had rolled over with me hanging out the window. The crazy things boys and teenager boys do is unbelievable.

Brian's Prefect was eventually written off when one day on his way to work on a dairy farm, he forgot to look for trains as he crossed the unguarded crossing on the farm. One of my uncles, Keith Hough from Collie, was driving the train, which was hauled by the largest of the steam engines in Australia (V class), when it hit Brian's car. After he stopped the train and ascertained that Brian was not hurt, he was amused by Brian's rant to him that he (Keith) was at fault and was trespassing on private property.

Janice Nash

When Janice was about seventeen years old, she successfully took part in a Miss West Coast beauty contest at Bunbury and was crowned Miss Bunbury.

One day when we were entering puberty, she told me she had to stay away from Uncle Ron, one of my mother's brothers. When I asked her why she told me that he had touched her breasts. Neither of us told our parents because even though nothing was ever said, we knew they would only tell us to 'just stay away from him'.

One day, decades later, while talking to Uncle Ted, Janice's father, I mentioned Ron's crimes and how disgusted I was. His response was "We all make mistakes, Robbie." I was gobsmacked.

Uncle Ron's reign of terror came to an end when an eleven-year-old victim told her best friend at school that he was having sex with her. The friend went home and told her mother, and she told the victim's mother, who went to the police. I attended the court to see if the mongrel got what was coming to him and was sickened by what he had been doing to the girl since she was five years old.

Disappointingly, but luckily for Ron, no other women came forward to testify about what he did to them as kids. As it turned out, he had molested most of my female cousins, nieces, and other girls. Not knowing Uncle Ron's history of deceit and debauchery, the judge sentenced him to fifteen years cut down to only five because Ron was a 'good citizen' in his town and had pleaded guilty at the outset.

Another sickening part to this is that Ron's wife, Shirley, and my mother both stood by Ron, saying: "If she didn't like what he was doing, why did she keep going back". This attitude worried me for years until I finally figured it out. To that generation, it must have been considered normal to be interfered with by family members. After much thought and remembering discussions of extended family, I realised that Mum may have been interfered with as a kid, and I had my suspicions of who the men were that likely interfered with her. I've also always been puzzled as to why my brother Barry visited Ron in prison. Barry obviously had his reasons, but nobody else in the family, apart from maybe Mum, ever visited him.

If stress and anxiety bring on cancer, then the young girl's father was another victim of Ron's treachery, as he developed cancer during these proceedings and died.

A few years after Janice told me about Ron's actions, while I was recovering from the bad motocross accident and still under rehabilitation, I was living with Janice and her family. We played darts on the back verandah and Janice would keep walking between us and the dartboard. After several ignored warnings, I threw a dart across her face as she walked in front of me, missing her by a few centimetres. She oddly didn't walk across there again.

I don't know what it is with girls and other people playing darts, but around the same time while playing darts on the back verandah at home, my sister Dixie kept going in and out the laundry door our dartboard hung on. After many ignored warnings, I lobbed a dart toward her feet. I miscalculated the speed of her feet because the dart ended up sticking up out of one of them. She too never repeated her annoying disturbance of dart players, and we were both lucky the dart didn't hit any bones, tendons, or nerves.

Johnny Hay

Johnny and I, as cousins, spent a lot of time together getting up to mischief, but extremely mild mischief compared to what some kids get up to these days. We made a batch of rotten egg gas and proceeded to place open bottles of it where it would most annoy people. The first bottle we put in the ute driven by a reporter for the *South Western Times* – nobody locked their cars in those days. The second we took into a private hotel in the main street of Bunbury – just walked up the stairs like we owned the place, found a vacant room and placed the bottle in a clothes drawer then walked out again without seeing anybody.

On a busy Saturday morning, as shoppers walked down the main street, we rode our pushbikes up the street on the wrong side of the road shooting people with our water pistols. Strange that nobody tried to stop or follow us. I guess people were far less uptight those days.

At Johnny's house one day, we entered the house through the downstairs door, through a bathroom where his older sister Helen was having a shower. He was in front of me and, as he went passed the shower, he gave the shower curtain a flick to open it a bit so I could have a look at his big sister. I didn't peek, knowing I'd get into trouble if Helen saw me peeking.

Another adventure Johnny and I had was to play chicken with cars. We started up the top of Stephen Street in Bunbury and tore down across Victoria Street, the main shopping precinct, dodging the cars going along it. One day I misjudged (maybe the driver saw me and slowed down) and I hit the car just in front of its rear wheel. Amazingly, my wheel didn't buckle, but it and the forks got pulled around ninety degrees and I flew over the handlebars. The poor driver jumped out and apologised as I righted the wheel and took off down the street without saying a word to him.

Speaking of playing chicken, a couple of mates and I used to stop our pushbikes across a railway line when a train was coming to see which of us would chicken out first and take off. I got a good laugh out of the sight of the steam engine bearing down on us with the whistle blowing loudly, steam billowing out with the brakes squealing. I was always the last to move.

Pat O'Brien

Pat is about seven years older than me and joined the Navy in 1958, so spent a lot of time away from home. While he was away being trained, his family moved from Collie to Bunbury.

On one of Pat's shore leave periods, he came home to Bunbury and I found him in the Forster orchard with two pretty girls. They were sitting either side of him and taking turns to kiss Pat, who was enjoying himself, of course, and I left. My imagination runs riot now, about what may have happened after I left them.

Glen Britza

"See you later, champ," I said as my cousin Glen turned to leave the room. I could see he was embarrassed by this title, but he had just won a state motocross championship on his 200cc Dot and I was overwhelmed by his talent.

I was nine years old and my eighteen-year-old cousin Glen was my hero. He sometimes turned up at our place on his smoky, loud two-stroke motorbike to babysit us while Dad and Mum went out. A fast-talking, lanky teenager, who always wore overalls, Glen was always ready to laugh and joke which was a personality I liked, and over the years I took on as my own.

For me, Glen could do no wrong and when his name appeared in the local paper because he had been fined for all types of traffic offences, I would read it out proudly to my family members. One offence I still remember was his overtaking another vehicle on the wrong side. I still don't have a problem with that one, if people want to drive too far to the right, why not overtake on the inside?

I rode my first motorbike at eleven years old at the old golf links in South Bunbury, with Glen. The bike was his 200cc two-stroke Dot from England, owned by Glen and assisted with maintenance by John Kirkpatrick. Wow, what a thrill and the excitement of the power at the twist of a grip was amazing. I must've grinned for a week after that, and now was really hooked on motorbikes.

Dot motorbike

In May of 1961, my mother received a letter from the President of the Bunbury Motorcycle Club asking for her permission for me to take part in motorcycle riding and maintenance training. Thankfully after much hassling and begging from me, she wrote a letter of compliance.

I joined the Bunbury Motorcycle Club (BMCC) as a junior member and was able to start racing on Glen's 200cc Dot – by now he had a new Greeves 250cc motocrosser from England.

I raced on the Dot, and his Greeves when I became more competent and was winning races against other juniors.

Me on Glen's Greeves waiting for a juniors' race to start at Hawkstone Park

Glen (on left) and John Kirkpatrick with Glen's new Greeves 1961

Glen built a motocross sidecar around 1961 and I immediately put my hand up to be his passenger (now known as a swinger). We went on to compete at Bunbury, Collie, Yallingup, and Harvey at a club level. The bike was an Ariel Red Hunter, a 500cc single-cylinder four-stroke with no rear suspension and only very short front suspension.

We raced at Yallingup on our solo bikes as well as the sidecar each year for some time. Being private roads that were open to the public, they had to close the roads to the public for one day a year or lose their 'private' concession, so they invited the BMCC to hold an event there.

The course started in the pine plantation opposite the *Caves House Hotel*, went across Yallingup Beach Road, down the hill and around the back of the hotel alongside a dam. We jumped off the dam wall, a drop of a couple of metres, and turned back up the other side of the hotel to Yallingup Beach Road again. The last part of the track was downhill on the newly tarred (with sand on top) road which, of course, was very slippery. During one lap, the sidecar slid sideways into the pit area, which was sand, and immediately somersaulted across the track in an enormous cloud of dust. We remounted and finished the race with no further mishaps.

The next race, as we were hurtling up the hill, I could see the sidecar wheel was going to hit the grader berm on the side of the track, so I sat on the mudguard to keep the wheel down. Unfortunately, there was a stump or large rock under the berm at that spot and the next thing I knew we were flying through the air. I ended up in a ditch with no feeling in my legs and I could hear Glen yelling, "Get this fuckin thing off me."

The bike had landed on him and had him pinned to the ground. My legs eventually regained their feeling and use as I dragged myself up out of the ditch using my hands and elbows. When we returned to the pits and I took my helmet and leather jacket off, I found, to my amazement, a print of the front tyre on the back of my helmet and the rear tyre on the back of my jacket.

We had an exciting race day at Allanson near Collie where we had three races to ride on the sidecar. Another friend, David Walker also wanted to ride passenger, which created a bit of a problem. I suggested that I do the first race and David do the first half of the second race and halfway through the race, we'd swap over for me to finish the race. We did that at the slowest corner on the track and went on to win the race.

One lap at that track, we were racing down into a left-hander on some sharp corrugations and my left foot bounced off the outside platform, under the sidecar wheel, and dragged me off the bike. I hung on as hard as I could flapping in the breeze and eventually, one of the bumps after the corner bounced me back into the sidecar. Glen was none the wiser as he hadn't noticed I wasn't there.

I only raced a sidecar with Glen but one off-season day while we were practicing on tracks around the bush I had a go on Ray Withers' outfit, but I didn't feel safe with him. Unfortunately, a couple of years later, Ray died after having a prang on his sidecar while going over a jump on the Allanson track. The bike landed upside down on his chest, severed his aorta, and he bled to death internally.

The Bunbury club organised an event near Harvey and

invited the Collie and lightweight clubs to compete. Part of the event was a relay race – each rider completed one lap, stopped before the line and a runner touched their bike and, running to the next rider and hitting him in the back, let him know to take off. I was the runner for our club, and nearly got bowled over by Edgar Renfree who didn't pull up in time. I just held my arm stiff and bounced off his number plate. I wasn't competing on a solo bike at this event but did compete with Glen on his sidecar.

I was also a runner in the relay race at the Herne Hill track for our club. This event was televised each year by the ABC, and they had an enormous trophy for the winning club. As the Bunbury club was the strongest club in those days, we came away with the trophy most years. Because the Bunbury club had won the event for most of the years it ran, the ABC presented the trophy to the BMCC to keep.

One day, we were testing the road racing bikes on the South West Highway for the upcoming road race event in Bunbury. I had a turn at riding Glen's bike and, when I got up to speed, the asthma spray I kept in my breast pocket was sucked out by the wind, never to be seen again.

The same day, one of the Renfree boys was also testing a road racing bike. When he returned to us, the local traffic cop from Bunbury had pulled in and was waiting for him. The poor cop was so excited to book one of us, he was ranting, "What's your name, Renfree? C'mon, Renfree, what's your name?" It took all my self-control to not laugh at him. Good thing he didn't get there earlier when I was riding, as I was only fifteen and unlicenced.

Apart from racing with him, I spent most of my spare time with Glen and did many kilometres as a pillion passenger on his road bike around Bunbury. That bike was a 200cc two-stroke Villiers-powered Excelsior. We never wore crash hats or any other protective gear, despite knowing the benefits of them through racing. I always wore thongs on my feet, one of which rested on the muffler as there was no footpeg on that side of the bike.

Our family was visiting Glen's family one night and I heard Glen go out on his bike and return twenty minutes later. He went into the bathroom and called me to give him a hand with something. He'd been out practicing in the dark for an imminent race on the 'around the houses' track at Glen Iris. Being night-time with very weak lighting on his bike and no street lighting, he'd hit a patch of gravel on the edge of the road and came off his bike. He needed me to hold a dressing on his arm while he bandaged it. It wasn't very pretty, but once again, I was in awe. And so began my disregard for minor injuries and pain. He'd ripped most of the skin off one side of his lower arm when he hit the bitumen, and went on to compete in the road race the next weekend.

Glen modified his motocross bikes to compete in the road races, quite successfully. He would change the motocross knobblies to road tyres, heighten the gearing and change his motocross handlebars to shorter 'clip-ons'.

One day I thought I'd make a sidecar for my pushbike, so armed with a few pieces of metal, timber, and a small bike wheel went ahead. By the time I got to Glen's place to show him my beaut creation, it had gradually fallen apart, and I had the lot in my arms when I got there. Glen, being the kind-hearted person he is, gathered some piping, clamps, and welder, and set about making a solid sidecar frame for my pushbike. Away I went, proudly showing off my new beast. It was extremely popular with my young friends, as I gave them rides on it, and, seeing the glee on their faces, made me feel like a hero to them. Being the only pushbike sidecar in Bunbury, it was a great point of interest to everybody.

After my Dad died when I was 13, I spent most of my time at Glen's place with his parents and siblings. It was a place I felt appreciated, liked, confident, and not threatened or intimidated. I was spoken to kindly and taught plenty of life skills without any sarcasm, getting picked on or belittled. I never slept there but was there reading Glen's motorcycle magazines early on the weekends, waiting for him to wake up.

One Saturday morning, we rode Glen's bike to the BP depot near the Bunbury jetty – I carried a 20-litre steel drum to buy some racing fuel for my bike. On the way back we went into a right-hand corner and Glen dropped off the side of his bike as if he was riding his sidecar, leaving me sitting up like Jackie with 20 litres of highly flammable racing fuel sitting on my knee.

I was riding my pushbike along King Road in Bunbury one night when I heard Glen's bike come up behind me. As he reached me, he grabbed the back of my seat and powered up the road, pushing me along. I had my lighting generator working on my front wheel for a change and, as we hurtled over the railway line hump in the road, the headlight glowed strong enough to light up half of Bunbury and then exploded.

We spent most Saturdays at the motocross track on 'busy bees', remodelling and generally maintaining the track and buildings. Glen worked for a Ford dealer (Dorsett Motors) in Bunbury and was able to borrow a tractor to do the heavy work. He also collected old engine oil from Dorsett's to pour on the track to keep the dust down.

Now, most of my mates were much older than me as I hung around with the riders from the BMCC; some taught me to ride and I later raced against them.

Glen and I were travelling south on Blair Street in his ute and where it crossed Clarke Street (now a roundabout), we collided with a car coming from our left, which should have given way. That car was driven by Mrs Stewart (the mother of another motorcycling mate, Keith Stewart) – it rolled over after the impact. Mrs Stewart had a bag of chook feed inside the car and a thermos of coffee she was delivering to a friend in hospital, both of which broke and combined to coat the inside of her car with coffee-flavoured chook feed.

I saw Keith Stewart on his scooter one day, hurtling around a corner in town. He was sitting backward on the scooter using his left hand on the throttle and right hand on the clutch/gear end of the handlebars. What a legend! Years later, Keith would become a city councillor.

My skin, and maybe my life was saved by two things in the collision: I had my arm out the window resting on the windowsill, and I wore brand new leather-soled shoes. Because I was almost thrown out of the car when the door flew open, my leather soles just skidded up the road as we slid sideways. With my left arm holding onto the door and my right elbow dug into the car seat with my bum outside the car, I rode the trip until we stopped. Luckily, the ute didn't roll over or I would've been a goner.

Dad introduced me to scrambles (now called motocross)

when I was about nine years old. He took me to watch my cousins, Vinty and Glen, compete. The first scramble he took me to was at Australind where Vinty was riding. I don't remember anything about that event except for the paperbark trees and the estuary in the background. But I do remember the next one at the old golf links, near the beach where now there are houses near the end of Mangles Street. In those days access to this track was by bush track only, and no road along the foreshore, as there is now. I also remember a 'one-off' track at Picton opposite the old Picton Primary School. This was known as a 'grass track' racing event as the paddock was flat with long grass.

The next track I remember is Hawkestone Park, which was on the western side of the drain alongside Hay Park. This track was used until the end of 1963 when the club acquired some land on North Boyanup Road. In 1964, we moved to Shrubland Park, which is the current track alongside the Bunbury Airport, (which was) built after our track. (I was competing on my own bike by then.)

As a teenager, I supplied sticks of gelignite with fuse and detonators for blowing trees out of the ground where we were building or modifying the tracks. Don Wendt – later to become my stepfather – was a bulldozer driver for WAPET in the Pilbara, and was employed to cut straight swathes through the scrub for seismic research. He stole the gelignite for me, and it was a great thrill being able to contribute something valuable to the club. I used to ride out to Hawkestone Park on my pushbike, the gelignite in a plastic bag on one end of my handlebar, the fuse and detonators in another bag on the other end of the handlebar. A lot of this ride was alongside the drain coming from the swamp, and I had fun jumping over the many humps on the track with no fear of the gelignite exploding.

One day after digging a hole under a tree and packing the gelignite into it, we lit the fuse and ran. One of the blokes lost a thong from his foot as we ran, and of course, went back to pick it up. Luckily, he didn't get hit by anything.

In 1963, when I turned sixteen, I could get an open competition licence which I did. We then competed on the sidecar in state rounds of the championships at tracks further afield.

Glen with me on sidecar

We used to take the sidecar onto the estuary mudflats at Australind when the tide was out to have a bit of fun practising figure-eights and just 'cutting sick'. Another place we took it was around the streets of Gelorup. In my hurry, I forgot to swap my new suede shoes for my boots, which made it very slippery on the wooden outside platform of the sidecar.

Another trick we tried on the sidecar, at Glen's suggestion, was riding it like a solo around one particularly sharp right-hander on the Hawkstone Park track. As we went into the corner, I sat behind Glen and he tipped the outfit into the corner with the 'chair' up in the air off the ground. It worked a treat, and we got around that corner quicker than any of the other sidecars.

I only ever once tried to drive the outfit with Glen in the 'chair'. When we got to the end of the straight, I couldn't turn the thing, so we shot off into the scrub at the end of the straight. I got off and told Glen he could have the bloody thing – I would stay in the 'chair'. Unlike motorbikes, sidecars are not turned by leaning over; you must push the handlebars around, which nobody remembered to tell me about.

My Cotton Cobra

Me on Glen's Greeves

I left high school the day before I turned fourteen, and never went back. I got a job, and began saving for a bike of my own. After two years and with the help of a loan from Uncle Don in late 1963, I acquired my very own brand new, Cotton Cobra. The Cotton was powered by a single-cylinder, twin carburettor, Villiers two-stroke motor called *The Starmaker*, which was used by all the British motorbike manufacturers of the day.

I used to practice my race starts and wheelies across our front yard, which created furrows across the yard where the back wheel would spin and dig up the grass and dirt. I also raced between the front and back yards going through a gate alongside the house. It's a good thing nobody tried to walk from the back of the house to the rubbish bins or gate, they would've been skittled.

In those days, most people still made their scramble bikes by converting road bikes – you couldn't walk into a bike shop and buy a purpose-built scrambler off the floor. I had to order the Cotton from *Clinton Bros Motorcycles* shop in Hay Street Subiaco and wait three months for it to be delivered into the shop. Other British purpose-built bikes being imported, mostly by Mortlock Motors, were Greeves and BSA.

Glen generously drove me up to Subiaco to pick up my new bike and drove me and my bike to events around W.A.

Glen has been a father-figure, big-brother figure, and mentor to me, and many other kids, over the years. He was always extremely generous with his time, loaning his bikes, and giving advice. Even now, when I'm 73 and Glen's 81, he offered me the loan of a vintage road bike to join his club on a ride on the roads around the hills of the Ferguson Valley.

Donna on my Cotton

My first event on the Cotton was at Manjimup in October of 1963, and I had some teething problems: a faulty ignition coil and a stuck throttle. I overcame the stuck throttle by using the kill switch every time I had to back off for a corner or jump. No way was I going to let a mere stuck throttle keep me from racing. We raced the sidecar at Manjimup too and I had a ball flying around that long track.

After Manjimup, we went to Rockingham for an event and, as I had just acquired my competition licence and was a virtually unknown quantity, I entered myself in the lower classes – it didn't take them long to wake up to me and place me in the A-grade race where I was trying to overtake Terry O'Leary, the then South Australian champion. On the last lap, I hit a small shrub with my gearstick which bent out of shape, so I had to retire from that race.

Then on to Forrestfield, a flat winding and smooth gravel track, where it was a lot of fun sliding around the corners. Here I was harassing Bill Watson, another champion, but my inexperience led me to run off the track and finish way back.

We also raced the sidecar the same day at Forrestfield, and that's when we came third in the Australian Short Circuit Championships. I suggested to Glen that if I threw myself at the sidecar wheel as we entered the right-hand corners, my shifting weight would put the outfit into a slide, letting us corner faster. We tried it and it worked a treat. The outfit that won the championship was a powerful road racing outfit brought over from the eastern states for the road racing championship a month later.

Mandurah had a great flat dirt track alongside the estuary where we raced that same year and placed second in the

West Australian sidecar short circuit championships. This was another track that was a heap of fun to race on – *hang on here, all tracks were a heap of fun to race on!*

At sixteen and seventeen years of age and spending most evenings at Glen's or Johnny Kirkpatrick's place watching them work on bikes, I began to do the maintenance on my bike which included dismantling the engine and rebuilding it. They were both great teachers and I learned a lot in a short time.

Working for a living in my teens

I had a couple of part-time jobs while still at school, including delivery boy for Pritchard's Chemist, and digging ditches for a plumber mate, Ray Withers who I raced bikes and sidecars against.

My first full-time job was as a delivery boy for Sherry's Chemist, delivering medicines and other stuff to customers. Graeme Sherry, the pharmacist, was a great bloke who I got on well with. Some of my other duties were to wash and polish the floors, wash up the beakers, mortar and pestles, and other paraphernalia, sweep the footpath out front and generally help out. I used to enjoy going to pharmaceutical suppliers on my pushbike to pick up orders. One of the suppliers was *Rumbles*, run by another older mate, Ray Duncan, who I also raced against on sidecars. While working for Sherry's Chemist, my brother Barry used to get me to steal condoms for him.

Another pharmacist, Kingsley Wake, came to work with Graeme as they got busier. Kingsley was younger and a great bloke. He employed me one evening to come to his place and steal bricks from the building site next door. I wore my leather jacket and ducked down out of sight when cars came passed. I think he paid me three quid and dinner with him and his wife.

I moved from Sherry's to another racing mate: Ray Truman's automotive spray-painting business where I rubbed down cars in preparation for his spraying them. This was not a good job in the winter as my hands were constantly in cold water using wet-n-dry sandpaper.

My next and last job in Bunbury was as a 'Call Boy' (officially Junior Worker) with the West Aust Govt Railways (WAGR). In this job, I worked three shifts with two other Call Boys to cover 24 hours a day. On day shift I carried out all sorts of duties such as cleaning windows, checking water levels in the overhead tanks that supplied water to the steam engines, turning on the water pump to fill them, counting the carriages filled with coal and where the coal came from, and delivering messages. To stop the steam engine water tanks from rusting out, I had to put soda ash and tannin at certain ratios in their water tanks.

All the mobile duties were carried out on a pushbike, and I was supplied with a waterproof cape, hat, and leather leggings in case of rain. Some duties took me from the roundhouse over the shunting yard – with many tracks to cross – to get to the railway station. Because there were so many trains parked and moving in the shunting yard, I had to walk across to the station. I did so by climbing between carriages even if they were moving slowly.

On the afternoon shift, I'd assist the Officer in Charge with the weekly Driver and Fireman roster and deliver messages. On both afternoon and night shift, my main duty as a Call Boy was to ride out to the homes of the Drivers and Firemen to knock on their windows to wake them up to go to work.

This could get a little difficult when two trains were going out simultaneously, and four staff needed waking up. Each Driver and Fireman had his own set time to be woken up for when he was due on duty. That meant they wanted to be woken up say, an hour or half an hour before due at work. When I had four to wake up, I had to stagger the times to suit where they lived and how long it would take me to get around to them all.

One afternoon shift when I had just started on the job, I was with another Call Boy. We were riding along a footpath back to the roundhouse, me in front of him. I noticed an old lady walking towards us on the path so rode off onto the road, expecting the other kid to do the same. Unfortunately, he didn't see her and ran into her, knocking her to the ground. We picked her up and apologized, even offered to carry her stuff to her house. But she didn't accept the offer and apologised to us for not seeing us coming and getting out of our way.

Another mate I raced against – Robert Bruce – was also a Call Boy. He sometimes pushed his father's car out of the driveway, stealing/borrowing? it to get around to call out the staff.

On night shift, there was often time between callouts so I would get some sleep, an alarm clock in my pocket to wake me when it was time to hit the road. I had a couple of places to sleep – one was sitting up in a steam engine on the driver's seat about 30cm in diameter. They were stuffed with horsehair, which, although not too comfy, were okay by me. When it was really cold, I would fire up a coal fire in the workers' hut and sleep on a long bench seat with my hands in the small of my back and my legs crossed so I didn't fall off.

One stormy night it was so windy I was at a complete standstill trying to ride against the wind, my cape acting as a sail trying to push me backward. The only option I had was to get off the bike, hide under my cape, and wait a few minutes for the gale to pass. Another night, about two in the morning, a meteor passed over Bunbury and completely lit up the whole town like it was daylight. I didn't know what it was, and at first, was a bit scared but reasoned that there was nothing landing as it petered out and just left a streak of light for miles.

An engine driver came in one night distressed because he'd run into a herd of cattle on the line on the outskirts of Bunbury. Some of them had their legs cut off by the train. We called the police to go out and shoot the damaged cows, but they took a long time and the next driver that came in was also disturbed by the sight. So we had to call the police again and eventually the cows were dealt with.

I got to 'fire' some steam engines and drive some as well, which was a bit of fun. I would also push the turntable around with a steam engine on, to line it up with a spot in the roundhouse for storage or maintenance.

There was a railway barracks in town where visiting drivers and firemen would stay while they were waiting to drive their trains back where they came from. It was my job on nightshift to light the kitchen fires and the hot water chip heater so the men could cook their breakfasts and have a hot shower.

To start the fires, I used the newspaper and kerosene supplied. I would screw up the paper, put it in the stove firebox with kindling, and pour half a king brown bottle of kero on it. While leaning on the opposite wall, I would hold a matchbox, scrape the match on it and throw it across the room at the firebox. It would go up with a lovely 'whoosh' that lifted the round plates off the top. They always dropped back into place. Then I'd go to the laundry and do the same with the chip heater, which was spectacular because the flames only had one way to go, straight back out the heater door in a large cube of flame. Spectacular to watch!

One of the other Call Boys and I used to race each other up the vertical ladders to the top of the water towers and back down. We also raced around the roundhouse on our pushbikes. One day I went too close to one of the long pits and was saved from falling headfirst into the pit when the end of the front wheel axle caught on the steel edge of the pit. That was too close for comfort!

I once pinched a pump off a pushbike parked in the laneway alongside Sherry's shop. Taking it to work, I held it on the railway line while an engine was being moved, just to see how much it would be flattened. I did the same thing with halfpenny coins, except of course I didn't hold them.

Mothers Day 1964

The last thing I remember when I woke up was flying toward a Banksia tree with a patch of white paint on it. The paint was to warn riders not to get too close to the tree which was on the edge of the track in the apex of a right-hand bend just after the tabletop jump. Unfortunately, the combination of loose, dry sand after the track had been 'ripped' to get rid of tree roots and an ill-handling bike, I lost control. The bike bounced to the left side of the track and I went sailing to the right, slamming into the Banksia at about 70Kph.

When I gained consciousness, I was surrounded by other riders and spectators. Glen was leaning over me.

I asked him, "Is my bike okay?" to which he replied, "Yes, it is."

I then asked him, "Is my left eye open?"

And once again, he said, "Yes, it is."

I said, "Well, I'm blind in that eye then," and slipped back into unconsciousness.

Meanwhile, my brother Barry and his girlfriend Pat, who was there spectating, both ran to his car and took off into Bunbury to get Mum.

"He drove like a madman, going through stop signs at 100mph, scaring the daylights out of me," Pat said.

They arrived back at the track with Mum before the ambulance got there, also from Bunbury.

After a few days, during which I drew closer to death, the doctors in the Bunbury hospital sent me to RPH so I wouldn't die on their watch. They obviously didn't know my spleen was ruptured and I was slowly bleeding to death.

On arrival at Royal Perth Hospital, I was met by Aunty Dora – or was she in the ambulance with me from Bunbury? I don't know as I was unconscious.

X-rays had been taken in Bunbury and when the doctor saw one of them, he asked, "What's that?" and pointed at the outline of my asthma spray. It had been in my pocket when I was x-rayed in Bunbury. I was conscious at the time and told him what it was, and he went off his brain because the Bunbury doctor hadn't made it known to him that I was asthmatic.

Mum was called twice to come to RPH from Bunbury because the doctors thought I wouldn't make it to the next day, but I fooled them and survived to ride another day.

The first operation was to remove my spleen and clean out all the blood enveloping my internal organs. I had a heap of blood transfused into me and one day, a nurse did something she shouldn't have and sprayed blood all over the bed, curtains, and floor. Very spectacular.

After I recovered from that operation, they placed a pin in my broken femur, cutting a large hole down my thigh so they could get their hands inside my leg to hold the ends of the bone together while they cut a hole in my buttock. Then they drilled a hole down my femur and hammered a long pin down almost to my knee.

My leg was then placed in a long splint that had a pulley and weight on the end. A pin was driven across and through my shin bone with a horseshoe-shaped device pivoting from the pin. The only way I could sit up was to grab the horseshoe and pull myself up because my stomach muscles had been cut to remove the spleen, and I had no strength.

As I started to recover, another young bloke and I were wheeled out onto the balcony overlooking Wellington Street for some fresh air and sunshine. He also had a leg in traction, and we delighted in pulling bits of cotton wool out of our traction devices, soaking it in our drinking water, and bombing pedestrians walking on the path below.

When I eventually left Royal Perth hospital and returned home two months later, I was annoyed to see in Mum's rag bag, my new tee shirt, jeans, and bright red jumper, all cut up. The medical staff had to cut the clothes off to x-ray me. The only things to survive the slaughter was my long leather racing boots.

Rehabilitation

Because of my prang in May of 1964, I spent eight months in the Melville Rehabilitation Centre on South Street O'Connor, this after leaving Royal Perth Hospital where I had spent eight weeks.

One of the patients, Terry Leam, who was in a wheelchair, was a smoker. He was a serial pest, so as he lit up I would flick the cigarette out of his mouth, much to his annoyance. When he'd had enough of my harassment and lectures about smoking, he'd rush at me with his wheelchair to cut my feet off with the wheelchair footplates. But I fixed him by putting my foot out to jam his footplates into the floor just in time to stop him. Sometimes he'd fall out of his chair and when that happened, I'd pinch it to go for a ride.

Terry had a Messerschmitt 3-wheeler car with a tiller for steering and all hand controls. We both drove on the roads in the bush opposite without rolling it over; much to my amazement.

Leigh Haines, a patient from Collie, was in rehab because of a head injury. He came into the mess for lunch one day carrying a bottle of milk.

Somebody yelled out, "Hey, Leigh, do you have to bring

your own milk?" and with that, Leigh threw it on the floor, sending glass and milk flying all over the place. Then he sat down for lunch as if nothing had happened.

Another patient, Ralph Eikelboom, a big Dutch bloke, also had a head injury, this one from a power drill through his forehead. I and others would greet him with "G'day, Fred," and he would respond loudly with "My name is not fucking Fred." Poor Ralph just stood around and didn't do much and was probably beyond rehab.

Christine Hardwick had some sort of spastic condition and had a three-wheel pushbike which I would often take for a ride. She loved me pushing her in her wheelchair while whistling the tune *55 Days in Peking* to her. Christine became a good friend; she came to my first wedding and gave us money boxes for our kids as they were born.

One girl, an epileptic, had a fit one day while walking along a path to the mess for lunch. Everybody just stepped around or over her. Because everybody was there for some medical reason, nobody took a lot of notice when this happened.

One of the young blokes was also epileptic and had 'grand mal' seizures which were quite violent. One night as I was returning from the laundry, he began to fit on the verandah. I could see what was about to happen so placed my laundry under his head to soften the blow when he crashed and continued to bash his head on the floor. He eventually came good but was groggy for some time – he and I just went on our way as though nothing had happened. The same bloke was a bagpipe player and would go off into the bush to practice. The first time I heard it in the distance I thought we were going to be attacked by a monster.

One interesting bloke I met there had tried to commit suicide with sleeping pills. He had large scars on his forehead, knees, ankles, and arms because he'd been asleep for six days and gangrene had set in where the pressure had stopped the blood flow. He was a quiet, nice bloke who I hope lived a long time after being discharged.

Nurse Jones, a gorgeous brunette, had a boyfriend whose car was parked overnight out the front of her house at the Centre. Somebody had put a brick behind his car wheel and when he tried to take off the next morning, he damaged the tyre. Nurse Jones blamed me – I never did find out who put the brick there, but it was a stupid thing to do.

Around that time, I'd had a shoulder reconstruction, and a large haematoma formed at the surgery site. Nurse Jones claimed she had run out of dressings and instead placed a large sanitary pad in my armpit to absorb the blood. Her idea of a joke to get back at me because I gave her a hard time I suppose, but I just went along with it without a complaint.

During my stay I had to have all my teeth removed as they were rotting at a fast rate, I think because all my calcium was being used up to mend my broken bones and none was left for my teeth. I had the operation and new dentures fitted at the Dental Clinic in Fremantle, all paid for by the Commonwealth.

Ray Sawyer was a bit of an odd bod and at home kept a flock of goats. He was alleged to have sex with them, but he didn't tell me about that himself, so I just took the story with a grain of salt. He got a job with his local Council after rehab, and the poor bugger got killed when the rubbish truck he was working with backed over him.

We had a real character – Keith Carr – another head injury casualty, who also had an orthopaedic brace on one leg so he didn't have a real good sense of balance. Keith spent a lot of time in the fruit and vegie garden where they taught patients about growing stuff. One day I wandered down there out of curiosity just in time to see Keith overbalance and fall backward into a pile of compost, much to my amusement of course. From that day, I gave him the nickname 'Compost', which stuck with him for the rest of his time there.

I started drinking at the Coolbellup Hotel during my stay at the Rehab Centre and often drank there with fellow patients. In those days the drinking age was twenty-one, and I was only seventeen, but nobody ever questioned me as everybody was very laid back about the law.

A bunch of us were drinking one night in the Centre's carpark and an orderly, Mr Lawrie, came by, so we hid our king brown bottle under the car. As he left us, he warned us to be careful of the bottle under the car, so we didn't get a puncture. What a nice bloke! Some other orderlies we knew would have wanted us thrown out.

We used to drink in the bush opposite the Rehab Centre where there was a grid system of bitumen roads from when the Army used the area during the Second World War. I heard they may have had accommodation in the form of tents along the roads. There were large holes around the area full of all sorts of rubbish, I assume left there by the Army. It's a shame I didn't think to explore the holes – I may have found some real treasures.

On a couple of nights, we set fire to blackboys in the bush opposite the Centre and watched them flare up beautifully. There were no houses around so nobody called the Fire Brigade, and we could enjoy the spectacle.

The metalwork shop was run by a great bloke, another real character named John Sarich. John was knowledgeable and kept all his charges safely in line. He used to go to his 'grandmother's funeral' every second Wednesday afternoon that oddly coincided with a horse racing meet. He allowed me to have my Cotton bike in the workshop to work on and make a stand for it, so it didn't need to lean on a wall.

Some of the patients put together a magazine called *Dodgers*, which I had a few entries in and I still have my copy after all these years. It was all typed out on an old typewriter onto Gestetner stencils and printed on a Gestetner printing machine. These stencils were a bugger of a thing because the typewriter keys cut through the stencils so the ink could go through during the printing process. If the typist noticed a mistake, he/she would patch the stencil with some pink liquid stuff, and when it was dry, type over it with the correct letter.

One of the boys in the Centre, Doug Jones, became a long-time mate. He had a Vanguard that he drove us around in. We took a trip down to Pinjarra and, on the way, got pulled over by a cop because Doug had been going a bit crazy around corners. This was way before breathalysers, of course, and the cop didn't even ask Doug if he'd been drinking, just what he was up to.

Doug said, "Sorry, sir, but the clutch is slipping," and the cop let us go on our way.

On the way home and with a bit more grog in us, the oil

light on the dashboard lit up so Doug said, "Just hold your thumb over it so I can't see it," which I did. Luckily, we got home without the engine seizing up.

Not long after I left the Centre, Doug, and others in his Vanguard, had been drinking in the bush opposite and got themselves nice and plastered. Leaving the bush, they turned onto South Street faster than they should have, and the Vanguard rolled over. Luckily, nobody was hurt, but some unfortunate soul who drove up didn't know that. What he saw was a car on its side, one bloke wandering around with only one arm and another bloke sitting on a log rubbing the stump of his previously amputated leg saying, "Aw shit, that hurts."

The bloke took off like a scalded cat, and the boys decided they'd better right the car and get back inside the Centre fast. Five minutes later there were blue and red flashing lights tearing up and down South Street looking for them. That's the only time I wished I'd been in a car accident – it would've been a fantastic experience to see the look on the bloke's face!

During the next few days, Doug cut the damaged roof off the car and welded a piece of water pipe across to hold the sides steady, thereby turning it into a Vanguard convertible.

Apart from boring basket weaving, leatherwork, and the like, my main learning involved metalwork where I learned how to use engineering machines like lathes, shapers, and mills. I also learned to weld while there.

Because of these new skills, I was placed with the Apprentice 1st Class Machinists at Chamberlain Industries for twelve months. Chamberlains made tractors of all types, and combine harvesters. All Apprentices served their first year in the apprentices' section and then three months in various sections of the factory. This gave them better knowledge of the different engineering fields and made it easier to choose their career path after graduating.

My favourite three months was with the testing department. Here they tested each tractor for power and torque on a dynamometer, then road-tested the tractors. The road testing used to be carried out on the public roads around the area until a steering wheel came off in a driver's hands and he crashed, receiving serious, multiple injuries. By the time I got to test the tractors, Chamberlains had built their concrete testing track in a large area out behind the factory. Boy, I had fun but got into trouble for scuffing the front tyres because I raced around the track as fast as I could.

One Saturday morning some apprentices were racing each other around the track on two of the tractors when one came unstuck. The tractor hit a patch of water on a corner from a rain shower the night before, slid sideways and fell over, being stopped by the large air intake device. Luckily, nobody witnessed it, so they righted the tractor somehow, drove it back into a workshop where they grabbed some new parts and replaced the damaged ones.

After spending twelve months with the apprentices learning all manner of engineering skills, I was sent to Wembley Technical College to do a 'trade test' to ascertain what my skill levels were. I was then given a two and a half year Apprenticeship based on my results of the test.

I met my first wife, Brenda, in the Centre. She was one of the Occupational Therapists employed by the

Commonwealth, and we had an illicit affair during my stay. After I was discharged, it became common knowledge among the staff and several of them attended our wedding. I'm sure if that happened these days, there would be hell to pay for her, even if it were discovered after I left the Centre.

Part Five

Bunbury Characters

Arthur Dunn

Arthur owned and operated the Forrest Theatre in Spencer St, South Bunbury, and built an open-air theatre with deck chairs alongside it. To stop people parking their cars outside facing the screen to watch the movies for free, he planted fast-growing pencil pines along the fence. Before the trees grew high enough, he would go out and ask people to move on, which they did. These days with all the aggro around, he'd have his head bashed in.

There was always a Saturday matinee with cartoons, a serial (Superman or such), and the main feature movie. There was an interval so kids could spend a bit more at his shop. Here you could buy choc-coated ice creams, a shilling (10c) bag of mixed lollies, packets of Findlay's salted peanuts for 6d (5c), Choo Choo bars, White Knight bars, Allen's Irish Moss Jubes, Peppermint Leaves, and many other goodies. He also put on games during intermission to keep the kids occupied and under control, and gave out prizes.

There were often holdups in the movie when the film would break, and we had to wait while the projectionist glued the film back together. This always created a loud uproar from the kids with comments like "Put a penny in it," and any other nonsensical things the kids could think of to yell out.

Sometimes a kid in the crowd would give out a loud fart which heralded some cheers and the comment "Bottle that one." Plenty of fun was had by all.

One day I decided to take a lackey band and some paper to the matinee to create a bit of a stir. I chewed a bit of the paper until it was soft then shot it at a kid a few rows ahead; it hit him in the ear. What a racket the bugger made, squealing and carrying on until the Usherette came along with her torch to see what was going on. Nobody had any idea where the missile had come from, of course, so I got away with that.

The first person in the ticket queue at the Saturday matinees got in for free, and it was always the same kid there first. That was Wayne Waldrodt, a spastic kid who rode a three-wheeler bike. Nobody minded him getting in for free because the poor bugger didn't have much else going for him.

Arthur must have had a contract to clean up the Hands Memorial Oval opposite the theatre after the Bunbury Show because he got lots of us kids to pick up all the litter and we got to get into the movies (flicks) for free the following week.

Jim Moon

Jim is the traffic cop I mentioned earlier. He used to pull me up at night when I was a teenager and tell me off for riding my pushbike without lights. He would sometimes pull me up three times in one night but never gave me a ticket.

Judy Moon

I also knew Jim's sister, Judy. She and I used to swap comics. Back in those days, we used to buy comics each week and, after reading them, we'd swap them for other comics that we hadn't read. Dad would buy *Phantom* comics for himself and *Donald Duck* and the like for us and suggested we swap our comics with other kids.

We used to swap a lot of goods in those days. I managed to swap an 'umbrella' lolly on a stick for a book called *Snugglepot and Cuddlepie*, a book I loved and kept for years.

When I grew older, I rode my pushbike to the flicks on a Friday night. We saw two movies, as well as *The Movietone News* and a cartoon. *The Movietone News* was a news broadcast like we have on TV, only on black and white film, so we got the news weeks after the event.

I would get the ticket selling lady to mind my pushbike headlight for me as it was given to me by my Grandad Britza and therefore was a valued possession.

My kerosene powered pushbike headlight

The headlight was powered by kerosene, had a red lens on one side, a green lens on the other side, and a thick clear lens on the front which cast a decent light beam. The headlight still has pride of place on the mantelpiece over our fireplace.

One night I went to the movies and ran into an older racing friend, Ray Buck, and his girlfriend, Anne Constantine. Ray grabbed my ticket, took it to the ticket booth, and paid a little more so I could sit with them upstairs in the 'posh' seats. They also shared their lollies with me – fantastic people who got married, are still together, and are stalwarts of the Bunbury Motorcycle Club.

While on my rounds as a Call Boy, I would sometimes see Ray's car parked at Anne's family house and ride up to talk to them. If I knew then what I know now, I would not have been doing that despite never finding them in a compromising situation, but I might have.

"Halfpenny Harry"

Harry ran a deli that also sold comics and magazines. He was known to rip the tops, including the title of the magazine off, and send the tear-offs back for a credit, but then still sell the magazines and comics. He sold a torn copy of a comic to my cousin Garry Britza, but his older brother Glen was awake to Harry and took the comic back for a refund.

Despite Harry being a bit of a crook, he was very personable, and I got on well with him. While working part-time as a delivery boy for Pritchard's Chemist, I earned £1-2 shillings and sixpence a week. Each Friday I banked the

£1, and on the way home would drop into Harry's shop and treat myself to a chocolate frappe, my only treat for the week.

There was an intellectually impaired bloke, Tony Salmon, who sat on a seat on the Bunbury Railway Station every day and said Hello to everybody going past; he'd talk to anybody who'd pass the time with him. He'd been there that long that people used to call him the Station Master, which I'm sure he would've loved. Each payday, the other workers on the station would get a pay envelope from the Paymaster, and each of them put a few pennies in it to give to Tony as his pay. He was over the moon about that.

Learning to Drive

In my day there were no such things as driving schools – we were taught by anybody who had a driver's licence. I never had driving lessons or advice as such; I just watched and took notice of how other people drove and learned from there. I had already been riding motorbikes for six years so it was only a matter of converting that knowledge to four wheels.

Of course, my favourite drivers were those who took risks and had a lot of fun driving, so that's the way I grew into driving. I had great mentors to learn from such as Glen Britza, Edgar Renfree, Don Collins, Bill Edwards, and Don Wendt.

Driving down to Cowaramup one Sunday for a scramble event on the town oval, we followed a Collie competitor in his car whose trailer was loaded with bikes. We came up to a slower car and overtook it without going off the edge of the narrow road, leaving a gap of about 75mm between my door and the other car's door, the front of Glen's ute about 50mm from the back of the trailer. I was super impressed, but I bet the driver we were overtaking nearly had a heart attack.

Don Wendt travelled everywhere in his ute with two 200 litre drums in the back, one full of diesel for his bulldozer, the other full of petrol for his ute. The drums were never tied down and Don drove like a demon, including cutting corners on all the right-hand bends.

When out with Don Collins, driving down the main street of Bunbury on a Friday or Saturday night while lots of people were window shopping, he had a couple of tricks to play. On a rainy night, he'd drive down the street in the gutter showering pedestrians with water. Other nights he'd drive down the same street and back off the accelerator, turn the ignition off for a second or two, then back on making an enormous bang when the exhaust backfired. A wonderfully loud bang bounced off the walls of the shops on either side of the street. Any veterans from the war walking down that street would've had a heart attack, I'm sure.

My first cars

My first car was one of the earliest VW beetles in Australia; it had a very small rear window and only one exhaust pipe. This model had a 1.13-litre engine and only one gauge, the speedo. So, without a fuel gauge, if you ran out of fuel, you just kicked over a small lever on the floor that turned on the reserve tank, which probably held about five litres of fuel. So, you never went away for a long trip or returned without re-fuelling beforehand. The headlight dip switch was like all other cars of the day, a push button on the floor you hit with your left foot.

That car only lasted seventeen days. One night returning from Armadale, where we went to get a burger from a caravan burger bar, we hit and killed a cow. Brenda was driving and, as we went around a bend on Armadale Road where it crosses Nicholson Road, there it was – a black cow on the road. Another driver had pulled up on the other side of the road and thought he was being helpful by flashing his headlights at us as we approached, which only took our attention away from the road and the cow. It would've been far smarter to have his lights shining on the cow. A few days later, I visited the farmer who owned the cow and managed to get him to pay for the car, which was written off. I then bought an FJ Holden.

My first car after colliding with a large cow in 1965

Crushed FJ Holden

My second car was the FJ Holden above, which I had for three months before rolling it over into some trees on the Old Coast Road. The FJ was 'souped-up' so went really quick – it was fun to drive fast everywhere I went. I was doing 80 miles per hour (about 130kph) around a bend on a sand section of the Old Coast Road when somebody had the audacity to come from the other direction. I had to move over a bit and touched the grader berm, then slid over the other side of the road, the car now on its side, into some small trees. The roof came down into the back of the seat and pushed me and my girlfriend, Brenda, (later my wife) down into the seat. I only suffered a small gash in my back, but Brenda broke her collarbone. The car was fitted with lap-sash seat belts, but we never wore them as it wasn't compulsory to do so.

I was devastated that Brenda was injured. When I got back to Aunty Hazel's place where I was living at the time,

Aunty Hazel and I were sitting at the dining room table talking about it when I broke down and cried.

I said, "Why did she have to get hurt? Why couldn't it have been me?"

Aunty Hazel responded, "You've been hurt a lot already; you don't need to get hurt anymore."

Brenda and I went on to get married in 1968 and our first kid (Tim) was born in 1971. Tim was followed by Cath in 1973 and Jamie in 1976. Tim and his wife Justine have twins, Oscar and Harvey, while Cath and her husband Michael have a son, Harrison. Jamie and his wife Sharon don't have kids of their own, but Sharon has two daughters, Verity and Kate from a previous marriage.

We have been blessed with these fantastic offspring. They are all gainfully employed, not drug addicts, are well-mannered, kind, have their own homes and are amazing parents.

Heaps of love to you all.

Acknowledgements

My gorgeous wife Chris, mentor, confidante, and encourager extraordinaire

Teena Raffa-Mulligan, author, multi-skilled writer, and my patient teacher, mentor and friend who has kindly led me through this adventure with only positive comments and praise

Aunty Lorna, Mum's baby sister, for the stories and insights into my parents

Aunty Betty, Dad's baby sister, for the stories of Dad growing up

Robyn Kenny, cousin, for the memories of growing up in Bunbury

Wendy Britza-Hay, cousin, for memories and photos of Dad and Nana and Grandad Britza

Sasha Wasley, author and cousin, for reading and critiquing my penultimate draft

Lucy Cotton, author, for reading and critiquing same

John Gardner, author, for encouragement to finish my book.

A massive thank you to all of you; it hasn't been easy battling the fear of failure and insecurities of writing a book. The next one will hopefully be easier.

About the Author

Rob Britza is an Australian writer of short stories. He has had two of his stories published in an anthology, which is in his local libraries, the WA State Library and the National Library of Australia.

Rob has written and had many articles with photos concerning local issues published in the Peel District of WA newspapers.

His first published writing was in the *South Western Times*, a Bunbury WA newspaper, when he was a junior member of the Bunbury Motorcycle Club. At thirteen years old, Rob was disappointed there was never any articles on his beloved "scrambles" sport, so he wrote his own.

The Dept of Parks and Wildlife WA use Rob's photos in their publications and on signs in their National Parks where he and his wife Chris have spent many months as volunteer camp hosts.

Rob's dry sense of humour shines through in his writings to keep his readers amused while successfully getting his point across.

www.ingramcontent.com/pod-product-compliance
Lightning Source LLC
Chambersburg PA
CBHW071623080526
44588CB00010B/1240